SEKXPHRA

SEKXPHRASTIKS

Jane Goldman

Dostoyevsky Wannabe Originals
An Imprint of Dostoyevsky Wannabe

First Published in 2021
by Dostoyevsky Wannabe Originals
All rights reserved
© Jane Goldman

Dostoyevsky Wannabe Originals is an imprint of
Dostoyevsky Wannabe publishing.

www.dostoyevskywannabe.com

This book is a work of fiction. The names, characters and incidents portrayed in it are the work of the authors' imagination. Any resemblance to actual persons, living or dead, events or localities is entirely coincidental.

Cover design by Dostoyevsky Wannabe Design
Interior Design by Tommy Pearson, Pomegranateditorial

ISBN 978-1-8380156-4-0

Preface

I have learned so much in these pages and felt held but also pushed and tugged and flipped, I have fallen through portals and glimpsed through doors ajar and touched sharp bits of glitter and followed the trail of other animals and had galleries blasted open for me when the world felt only my room and stupid tesco. It's a whole commons of names and contributors, the histories of various collaborations, intimacies, solidarities, rituals. Full of shimmers and echoes, this book is doing something radical with citation—a sending up in that kind of Fred Moten way, a feminist practice as per Sara Ahmed, a queer phenomenology maybe, but it also feels like a distinctly kind of Scottish sense of sociality, occasional chorus, that can reach from the pub to the jostle of historical voices and with the elegance or distance, difficulty of high theory brought to a 'bitchy tapestry' (Lisa Robertson) of lyric. An embrace of building something rich and generous, this is so much a work of *uplift*: towards the work of others, towards happenings, and like poetry itself as that happening, kinetic, unpredictable, full of glitches and swerves and figures. *SEKXPHRASTIKS* is a derangement of the senses as well as a sharp intersectional appraisal of encounter, often going beyond the human. I think that's in line with Tessa Berring, Bernadette Mayer, but also like Dorothea Lasky's kind of ritualistic shout-voice that is wild and spirited.

Maria Sledmere

Contents

TUTELAGE

NONAGE

COVIDCODA

for Robbie, twenty-one
and all you sonsie bitches

SEKXPHRASTIKS
a poetics of sekx, ekphrasis, and tiks

kx: mortal osculation, elusive, intimate soma-chromatic space :: phonics, orthographics in collisions, sing inky kicks in glitch plosive slippages (voiceless velar stops, voiceless palatal stops, voiceless velar non sibilant fricatives, voiced alveolar sibilant fricatives, unvoiced alveolar sibilant fricatives sound from throat tracts, a kerning cuts silent page diamonds) :: k marks itself, also universal play (simply one thousand or potassium, cumulus or carat, a measure of sun mass, a quantum number, a spatial factor, a facility for form, a terrified canid before the bleak law whose baffling fate is state judicial murder, k is the gallows, k is a lie, k queers) :: x marks itself, also excess (simply ten or any number, universal sex chromosome, a generation, a multiplier, 'adult' classification for explicit erotica or violence, a universal, transferable wet signature (the unlettered's letter), x precise cartographic location, a name withheld or lost, an unknown, unnameable, undetermined entity, unfixing fiction, a variable, a deletion, a kiss).

sekx: a poetry that aspires to a form of creativity with all the eddying charge of the pleasuring erotic intimacies of sex, where the term sex is liberated from the archaic sense of assigned binary biological reproductive categories.

ekphrasis: a rhetorical device that speaks (describes, explains, thinks, studies, argues) works of visual, plastic art, and/or is a form of visual, plastic art :: a poetry on intimate terms with other works of art, where art is a verb, universal to everyone living.

tiks: bodily spasms, poetry spasms, (poly)tics, poetry-making as lived, embodied, social experience, poetry born of a sense of extreme presence.

SAPPHO 1

calling all glitter arsed slay queens foam divas
meaning you you cunning wee cunts i-i beg you
don't you crush my heart to new lows of grief you
bitches it's passion

but get here right now if you give one toss
take my calls like you did last time long distance
no holds barred—you all fired in—bailed on your boss
golden girls you came

helicoptering in on groovy gold blades
down you flew top speed toward melanine earth
whirling whisked like concupiscent fruit smoothies
earth sisters mid-air

you got here so fast you bountiful bitches
beaming with good looks you soon asked me what's up
with you this time? why the torn face you daft cunt?
when i-i called you

what is it that i-i most longed to come next
for my crazy lust? who must be seduced now?
who's the honey to push now into your charms?
who hurt you Sappho?

if she's running now she'll be on the pull soon
patches you now she'll do all the texting soon
not in love right now she'll be all loved up soon
fuck what she desires

come to me right now cut me free from grievous
suspicions fulfill for me my fantasies
carry out all my hot heart longs to get done
bitches give me strength

SEKXPHRASTIKS: EXHIBITS

LANDRESSY STREET ARTEMISIA

∧

what is wormwood good for
bitter water star you know

all about tarragon keep an eye
out for catherine who knows

every girl's stuprum her own wheel
no you'll never give up to daddy's

man this girl pledged to thumb
screw it is true it is true it is true

how you scratched and tore
while he forced and gagged

you cut at his cock you slit
out a piece of his flesh you

spat it all out it is true you
know all about tarragon

∧ ∧

shady and amorous let all
our flowers fall for your slow

eyed self-convergence loose
props broken about to fall

away your robes are slipping
your bonnet barely balances

all this heaviness topples toward
us pinned now by frown dimple

barely balanced your bonnet
slips your frond tips your filet

falls about broken props loose
eyed let converging selves fall

slowly your flowers are falling
into our laps amorous and shady

∧ ∧ ∧

we too it is true it is true
know all about tarragon

let fall crones zine black sisters
lesbian avengers disability dykes

working class queers zine yes you
have struck a rock women are

strong society went wrong what
to do if the police raid trans diva

magazine speaks minds hysteria
photoworks picture our bodies

our futures bitter water stars we
know what wormwood is good for

WHAT IF THE MAJOLICA PLATE

what if the majolica plate
that is so firmly set in the wall of the dining room
display and is posing itself so self-consciously in
the sealed empire of objects glazed as it has to be
with opaque tin enamel entirely concealing the
colour of the clay body (the clay body entirely
concealed) is not after all the problem is not after
all the origin of all our tea-table oppressions is not
after all the negentropic source of all our woes the
very emblem of infinitely many muddled ways
the very ways that things will always go towards
muddle and mixedness?

what if a majolica plate
is as such the many muddled ways towards muddle
and mixedness and is in fact the precise
information that is a difference and a difference
that is a relationship a difference that is a change
in the relationship and a change in the relationship
produced by its negentropic effect without the
necessity of making a final intervention without
the necessity of giving up on tea-table thinking a
tea-table thinking that makes a happiness a
happiness that must think peace into existence?

what if a majolica plate
has after all been conceived as a pot for a definite
purpose and is striving towards a new mixedness
of unity and spontaneity and simplicity of form
and has in fact made itself as simple in its form as
it has to be and is only as muddle patterned as it
has to be to be itself enduring and full of quiet
assurance emanating itself from myriad vital
forces behind a clay body a clay body that is
flowing through the processes of its own making
as glazed as it wants to be with opaque tin enamel
entirely concealing the colours of the clay body
(the clay body entirely concealed)?

what if a majolica plate
is a pot for a definite
purpose simply formed
to cast a speech bubble?

FRUITMARKET TRIPTYCH

^
bounded
morphology
of sign
        bounded
        morphology
        of screen
glazed circuit
glazed circuit
glazed glaekit
                        no other glazier's
                        paint-coating
                        offers this level
                                of slickness
                                when cured this
                                ceramic pro
                        technology
                        will transform
                        itself   glazed transparency
                                              cracks
                                              glazed opacity
                                                    this bought
                                                    morphology
                                                    of circuit
                                              is bonded
                                              opacity
                                              is bonded

opacity
cracks
transparency
    transparency
    cracks
    opacity
opacity
cracks
transparency
      get over
      yourself
      do
         look to the storm torn
         roof of fruitmarket
         look for
      swamp floated
      concupiscent
      cupola
           radiant copula
           chroma cupola
           prismatic lux fruit
              chroma
              cupola
              chroma
           a bliss storm
           is coming up
           castlehill

＾ ＾

bring a burning
gondola
of fenders
　　bring fire
　　fountains of
　　stravinsky
bring three pots
more for the
poorhouse
　　　　　i-i see
　　　　　castlehill
　　　　　a volcano
　　　　　　　i-i hear
　　　　　　　castlehill
　　　　　　　a volcano
　　　　　castlehill will
　　　　　castlehill will
　　　　　fall
　　　　　　　　castlehill will
　　　　　　　　rue its ills
　　　　　　　　will rue them all
　　　　　　　　　　castlehill will
　　　　　　　　　　erupt into yes
　　　　　　　　　　yes will erupt
　　　　　　　　this esplanade
　　　　　　　　a lava of chroma
　　　　　　　　polymer bliss

well might you
tremble
tremble
    cut yourself out
    in silhouette
    like kara walker
serve dinner
like judy
chicago

        take a carless
        drive on foot
        to a foodbank
            sit in your piss
            sleep every night
            on icy streets
        beg three pots
        more for the
        poorhouse

^ ^ ^

opaque screen
cracked sign
go on run
 everything
 inside you is
 broken open
run run run
like a caryatid
sprung into hope
    by nancy spero
    one foot planted
    in neon painted
     eden a neon
     painted eden
     eden city
    this city sets rock
    on fire blazes
    into chroma like
      a ca mcnairn
      the scott
      monument
       is her brazier
       yes the scott
       monument
      is a kiln it
      becomes chroma
      a yes chimney it

is a kiln it
stokes this pyro-
chroma bliss
        this esplanade
        a lava of chroma
        polymer bliss
well might you
tremble
tremble
                    what is a brass founted
                    foxglove that boaks
                    a spouting serpent
                        to jonet barker
                        margaret lauder
                        agnes finnie
                    helen pennant
                    to hundreds others
                    listed not listed

                        a foxglove a snake
                        a pair of brassy
                        hands of healing
                            back handing
                            an evil eye
                            hedging all bets
                        in the dual significance
                        the dual purpose of
                        many common objects

centuries of stony inquiry
into the cause and seat
of castlehill's fires the names
    of all its dead and who
    was responsible for
    such failures and was
the response adequate—all
answered by a two-faced brass
foxglove that boaks a snake

        let the blazing
        esplanade speak
        yes the blazing
            esplanade speaks
            yes she says
            belt up
        yes belt up do there is
        no monument no
        sign there is no pun

                cracked enough
                there is no *crack*
                punned enough
                    no screen
                    no mirror
                    no sign yet
                to bring back
                the choked
                revive the burnt

NEW BEGINNINGS ARE IN THE OFFING

^

i-i like scotland and scotland
likes me no use looking
in un-saving silence
for the single catastrophe

      chained events beyond
      anchorages beyond
      inshore navigational

dangers new
fangs are always
first giants between

      grey felt hat
      (not a stage
      but a border)
      silent morphology
      of joseph beuys

also somewhere else
shooting his left profile
warmth ferry of sorts

and bronze nose
(not a stage
but a border)
silent morphology
of greyfriars bobby

also somewhere else
looking into the offing
warmth ferry of sorts

another stray bobby

is barking the last
kantian for greeting
the lost war prisoner levinas
watchful other : watchful for the other

another stray beuys

is disembarking the first
fat felted transatlantic
flight stretchered for

a reckoning to be made with the coyote
watchful other : watchful for the other

∧ ∧

o bobby and bobby and beuys the world
is gone as if with clara we are losing all
vivacity let us no longer care who
among us has the necessary brains to
universalize the maxims for drives
let us carry each other into the offing

through lavender filters through
willful sun-filled lavender filters

        let us spin and dive and piss
        on the wall street journal
        let us spin and dive and piss
        on the daily record
        on the daily newsfeed
        digital media is on fire
        with poetry's piss

let us enlarge the idea of art
let us make social sculpture

o bobby and bobby and beuys the world
is gone as if with clara we are losing all
vivacity let us no longer care who

among us has the necessary brains to
universalize the maxims for drives
let us carry each other into the offing
o bobby and bobby and beuys fear not
the bitches are coming coyotes we're

already here
world gone we're
pissing
with
gertrude + basket + pinka + virginia + frida + mr xolotl +
cliché + dorothy + june + amigo + cayenne pepper + donna
+ gaga + asia + (yes blackie + ca)+ eileen + rosie too
+ all kinds of necessary enchanters

watchful others : watchful for the others

^ ^ ^

every cunt ein künstler

GREYFRIARS BOBBY

now
touched
for luck
like Montaigne's foot
    his bronze cast nose
      all rubbed
       down
    to its shiny
    still it pierces

    the dreich

    this dis-
    appearing
    slowly nose

    our very
    beacon of

    the virtual

    subjectivity

    of pethood

SEVERED

shag-dog
earth dog
pretty little sky
dog
leapt between
hydra-headed mary
hydra-mary head
less a cleft neck
a pluri-serpent
salome some cleft
necked pluri-serpent
salome but john
the corpse
had him washed
clean the dog
imbrued with
mary had settled
between her clothes
between her cleftness
a dialogue in blood
washed clean the dog
was either burned
or washed clean or
washed clean the dog

was carried away
and washed as all
things
caravaggio must
mary queen of medusa
mary queen of gorgons
each thing she touched
was either burned or
washed clean then
given
away or sold the dog
was given away
to a french princess
condition the death
of a league of
nations the death
of a chromatic
libertine a gyno-
chromatic you
must send the peace
of nations as well as
baptists to incite
to leave death of
country a dialogue
in blood was soiled
cinematic mary

voltaire napoleon
marx and her shoulders
for fear someone
might dip a piece of
nations you must send
them to me in baskets
keep very warm hydra
headless headed
pluri-serpent
soiled with chroma
philia condition
being imbrued with
mary's blood
dialogue
salome john
the severed
in baskets
kept very
warm
hydra headed dog
basket warm
with mary's
blood washed a dog
a pretty little dog
a skye dog
a shag-dog

basket warm
a pretty little
    earth dog

ANDREW AND THE HANDS
(AT THE HUNTERIAN)

i-i'm stepping in from sunlight hurrying past so as
not to inspect again too closely the gravid

uterus and those wooden forceps and the never un-
wrapped so in excellent condition body of Lady

Shep-en-hor's mummy past principles of beauty
past horned screamer past shark's tooth (and this

is one of those teeth) past birds' nests in mid
nidification past phases of other animals'
architecture when

the hands

arrest me

(oddly all three gleam) in a tender buttery nip this trio
of polished wooden prosthetics produced by craftsmen

employed by the Yarrow Company Pattern shop in
Glasgow as patterns to allow (as a matter of fact)
disabled service

men and women at the Erskine Hospital to
manufacture artificial limbs for the casualties
returning from service

in World War One already melancholy they stir up
the queerest of steers to me to hurry on past
the opaque

Mona Lisa in Salon Six of the Louvre past all else
of its pleasures in the louche Uffizi too a steer my
friend Andrew first gave me

in 77 (so perfect he is texting me right now to say
what we always silently knew that he prefers
boys): go to the hands of the Titians

the ungloved saturnine index of the young sexy
Man with a Glove points downward unwarring
into the depths of a peaceful earth the satyr
discovers

himself cuckolded by the sleepy Venus del Pardo's
own earthy hand she is singing with wide-eyed
Venus d'Urbino with Nicki Minaj Beyoncé too

i-i'm feeling myself

IF MA HILLYBILLY
(358,000,000 results) is a feminist
   i-i don't want to be a feminist

^

st salome in her study finds sympathies
almost entirely now with clytemnestra
our sisters maenadistas our rosy
gorgonistas our daughters listen please do
listen we need to talk about ma
anna blume ma is not rosa luxemburg
ma is not mary wollstonecraft ma
is not angela davis ma is not
simone de beauvoir ma is not
julia kristeva ma is not
camille paglia ma is not
emma goldman ma is not
hélène cixous ma is not
johari osayi idusuyi ma is not

^ ^

ma hillbilly has unsexed herself
on foundation wads of salaries played

by sadly rabid & the guitarists ma
for two hundred grand a minute unleashed
the sadly rabid hard cheese disks ma
a shears-mammal of sorts tick-tock
sliced out the succulent labia cut out
the quick of a freaked nation like a slit cork
as any last duchess would say
   if everywhere eyes could speak
meanwhile euphoric ma through dripping
   severed
veins direct to camera ma says tick-tock look
we came we saw he died tick-tock venomous
ecce venimus vidimus periit tick-tock as if under
impartial surgical gaze a glistening ruby glans
just withers or serenely sheds
   her juicy fibro-vascular cap
slips off that very spot of joy a gadfly leaping
   from her own creaming
corpora cavernosa or solemnly submits to the rule
   of sadly rabid pa the slit
of ma's blade without agony without a struggle
do not spit this gristle milk for thieving metaphor
thinking to distance its orientalism knowing fine
   the slit
was a home cure of pioneer shrinks for hysterical
psychosis or psychotic hysteria & the swivel-eyed

         snivel
as shagpoke whipple enters the tent (a sluggardly
buzzard did veer its keel at my windscreen today
its full speckled beige span idled back to a glancing
         clip
is no portent of the whipple) is no excuse
so ma's over-stuffed shriveled out vaginiferous
boiled felt fawn suit so nicely buttoned at the
         wrist
can brag of having sat there in the driver's seat
for the full thirty-eight minutes (a cool seven
         point six
million dollars for sadly rabid and the guitarists)
         in the situation room
in intense honour or honour simulation (so very
         ma)
since that's what to ma honour looks like where
         even
the very subtitles of the inevitable and irrefutable
indicting documentary that so soon ensues are
spelling out ma's proud role a smooth lubricated
cock in the establishment military machine
talking doll-baby in a boiled fawn felt baby-suit

∧ ∧ ∧

our sisters maenadistas our rosy
gorgonistas our daughters listen please do
she waits until her new mom caresses her
the more your little one talks to baby the more
words and phrases she will learn and repeat
ma's example ma role-model ma mentor tick-tock
look we came we saw he died tick-tock

if ma hillybilly (358 million results) is a feminist
                    i-i don't want to be a feminist

WOOLFENSTEIN

i-i too feel weighed down by the whole
                              of gertrude stein
pressing into the syntax of this sentence pressing
its pressing syntax into this feeling
                              that the difference
is spreading is the difference spreading
                              the difference
spreads throned on a broken
                              settee attended by jewel struck
mermaidens who sit well in the difference
                              not drowning
they are not drowning but diving into
                              the wreck floating on deviance
fluttering with the tips of little fingers not yet
                              open not yet open
feeling tomorrow like we feel today feeling
                              tomorrow following bessie
swimming up to wave after wave with us
                              swimming up to say welcome
to hurry yes welcome to hurry that is
                              a sentence soon we will all feel
the weight of the whole
                              of gertrude stein soon we will all know

welcome to hurry welcome she is not heavy she

is our sister

ROLL OVER MALBODIUS

tell maboos the news
alice blue gown is all
mine all is my vanity
vanity is so my all
i-i am every wedding's
bride every funeral's
corpse you go try run
a country you'll never
control this daughter
this kimono kills fascists
so adore it i-i wore it
it's a lie it wore away
silk worms are all for it
now on your way out do
turn off that fake gold
dripping tap knock your
self out why don't you
burn the place down
what do i-i care don't
for one minute think
i-i'm not contracepted
no son of mine caught
dead beheading gorgeous

gorgons if looks could kill
mine will have to do here
hold my puppy i-i need to
go piss then primp

ST CLARE & ST FRANCIS VISIT SERCO

> And anybody listening to any dog's drinking
> will see what I mean.
> —**Gertrude Stein**

i-i'm bathing mastoids i-i'm
bathing love i-i love
in felonious web nests
a sow sumen of sorts
so belly up go to the end
of all query (you are
a doll) join me right here

fucking the choreo-
graphy budding with nest
nipplets better than worry
your little lilac mastoids
a no-show is mere fissi-
parous irony (they are
not joking) war is their biz

fat ploughmen have ploughed
into your data plan crops
we can't shield children from

strictly bifurcating irony
o the fissiparous irony
of their bifurcating ironies
try to see her new film

because of your red mouth
i-i'm bathing in love two-
sided i-i'm your one small
quantum mechanical demon
gender redistributor now
inductile flash violet for yes
now please re-imagine all

that nature on your she tv
suck up some semiotic manner
summon up a sumen somatics
adjust uddery semantics re-
direct your symbolic
insignificance out out it goes
the fissiparous irony

fresh beastings taste queer
talk about this veiled scene suck
deep into our common word
docs does anger peak anger
troughs i-i'm bathing mastoids i-i'm

bathing love try to see her
new film i-i'm your money i-i'm

your bread your sumen is
she trying to latch irony it's
the prisons service serco
employees who appear
as humane and thoughtful
people these are vignettes
to boost staff morale [yarl's
wood lol] so do let's try
to see the moll's new film

franky suckles clare—aye right
just listen to any dog's drinking :
this land is bitches' land
some bitches have milky tits
free-flowing egalitarian dugs
some bitches have big milky bottles
free-flowing silicone and latex teats
breast feeding is a social praxis
it must be learnt by hominids
any mutt can muster a mother's milk
franky is patriarchy's suckling
metoynym—franky has bitch tits
(there is a difference : spread it)

ARTEMESIA GENTILESCHI

has whelped nancy spero (at last)
long-dead fruit bowls is some mother
art intones something on the still
edge of her i-i am her executioner

i-i am on edge of mother into art
this allegory assassin has sprung
not fully formed out of nancy spero
vengeance over fruit effect is self

portrait the hands speak strong
as a mother as artemisia
gentileschi is to nancy spero
executioners of all these dead

metaphors lucretia is the allegory
harlot embrace me the allegory
terrorist always refuse stupor mundi
sisters mothers always refuse

stupor mundi these our dead sell
mere symbol resistance is blood lover
to a fatal woman is artist survivor
a blank bitch is canvas survivor

painter is painter pares painted
vindicational galleries will live
asking us to hold we must carry
the startling strength of her work

strength wherever a box
shows a shadow

MY ALPHABET BEGINS WITH C

C is for Colin Herd ⎫
C is for Daisy Lafarge ⎭
who make poetry things happen

C is for the CCA
    & for CAConrad ⎫
    & for Sophie Robinson ⎭
 who read beautiful poems in the CCA last night
 who will read beautiful poems tonight in:

C is for the Embassy Gallery
 C is for Sophie Collins ⎫
 C is for Caspar Heinemann ⎭
 who read beautiful poems in the Embassy
Gallery last Sunday

C is for all of yous here today
C is for Sappho

This is what Caspar Heinemann said in the
Embassy Gallery last Sunday
about Sappho:

> 'When Sappho says "muse" it means
> something like "poetry ghost" which is
> to say the muse is not the object or the
> subject but the facilitation or maybe the
> praxis'

which may be to say what Woolf is saying:

C is for 'continuing presences'
 C is for 'the cross-roads'
   & for Shakespeare's sister:

> 'this poet who never wrote a word
> and was buried at the cross-roads
> still lives. She lives in you and in me,
> and in the many other women who
> are not here tonight, for they are
> washing up the dishes and putting
> the children to bed. But she lives;
> for great poets do not die; they are
> continuing presences; they need
> only the opportunity to walk among
> us in the flesh'

C is for continuing presences in this room
   in this Embassy Gallery, once the studio
   of Caroline McNairn

C is for art space

C is for Julia who in the 1990s made art
   in this her sister's room in the mornings

C is for Caroline who shared this art
   room with her sister

   is for Caroline who made art
   here in this room in the afternoons

C is for the 369 Gallery & for Andrew Brown
   & for Hugh Collins who loved Caroline
   & were loved by her

C is for the Traquair House Studio where
Caroline made art until 2010

C is for Caroline C is for Ca

SEKXPHRASTIKS: (SOMA)TIKS

A SEMINAR RITUAL FOR CACONRAD

by Jane Goldman and Colin Herd

ice pigment glitter :: turmeric jasmine fire

BOOK:
CAConrad, *While Standing in Line for Death*
   (Wave Books, 2017)

SEMINAR ROOM:
Table covered in White Cloth:
  Table Centre:
    Ice Trays
    Single Tea Light (lit)
    Boxes of Matches
    Wipes

  Places Set:
    Colour Tabs
    Glitter
    Unlit Tea Lights
    Single Copy Student Poem (face down)

Side:

> *Bucket + Turmeric + Large Bottle of*
> *Water + Jasmine BB + safety-pins +*
> *word cards Extra Copies of all Student*
> *Poems*

PART ONE: ice pigment glitter

> **JG** Reads **'Poetry is a window [...]'**
> from paper; places paper on table adds
> pigment tab + ice +glitter

> **CH** Reads **'There Is No Prison/ Named Love'**
> from paper; places it on table; adds
> pigment tab + ice +glitter

> **All** In turn read the poem from the paper
> in front of them; place it on table; add
> pigment tab + ice +glitter
> **All** read simultaneously: **'Time Will/ Not**
> **Nurse You'**

PART TWO: turmeric jasmine fire

> **All** Don outdoor clothes; take to
> outdoor garden venue:

2nd copy of poems + tea lights
(weather permitting)
JG & CH Take matches + bucket +
turmeric + large bottle of water

OUTSIDE:
All Light tea lights (weather permitting)
All Read poems simultaneously; put
poems in bucket
CH & JG Pour on some turmeric; burn
the poems; retain ashes

RETURN TO SEMINAR ROOM:
All:
Mix ashes + jasmine bb into ice table poems
Read simultaneously **'There Is No Prison/ Named Love'**;
Scoop wads of ash poems into cups (for bathing in later);
Pin to clothes words taken from **'There
Is No Prison/ Named Love'** Take notes in silence
Write Poems, Read Poems, Discuss
Exit wearing words and carrying ash poems

AT HOME:
Bathe in the ash poems
Take notes
Write poems

ice pigment glitter   ::
tumeric jasmine fire

> tumeric
> in fire pigment
> on ice glitter glitter every
> where smoke glitter ice colin
> is giggling a tea light glisters flickering now
> in studio   now in seminar how
> long in the windy garden
> of the night a bucket full of
> poems burnt beacon of
> poems alive in tumeric
> alive in ashes the soil meets
> sparkling water bubbles flew
> over the soil was so moist
> and the way we all read keeping
> present present   i-i hear
> present present present at
> least four maybe five times
> back in the seminar the same
> present present echo we stroll into
> night strolling into the night
> strolls now into the table
> so many flickering faces
> around our floating table

of tea lights all aflicker glistering tiny
flames   embracing admix
of ashes   ice jasmine
pigment glitter soil we
speak poems with pulpy
tongues alive in glitter we
gather in these
glitter phials
flame candles
we rescued
from the
soupy

p

o

e

m

SEKXPHRASTIKS: REVOLUTION

REVOLUTION IN REVON STREET
REVOLT IN GRUBNIDE

a poemplay for Colin Herd
by Jane Goldman
inspired by & adapted from
Nathanael West's
adaptation of
Eugene Jolas's
adaptation & translation of
Kurt Schwitters' poemplay
Revolution in Revon

First performed for Poets Theatre at Hidden Door,
Edinburgh, 1st June 2016

CAST

Merzdogman   Nick-e Melville

Intra-dialogic Directions Focaliser/
Mr Melanie Dimble Pothook   Colin Herd

Child	Iain Morrison
Mobymarysittingwomen: Mary Beton	Lila Matsumoto
Mary Seton	Sam Walton
Mary Carmichael/ Young Poet	Roween Suess
Anon/ Anna Mhairi Nicola Fish Blossom	Daisy Lafarge
Father/ Policeman	Mike Saunders
Crowd/ Mob	Tom Betteridge
Crowd/ Pal	Emilia Weber
Dr Michael Roger Screwtop Burke Walter Amadeus Dimble Thatch Blair Pothook	Sam Riviere

Elvis M. Stranger	Sophie Collins
Props	Roween Suess
Fish Bearer	Jane Goldman

REVOLUTION IN REVON STREET
REVOLT IN GRUBNIDE

:

Scene: Revon Street, Grubnide city centre.
A child is playing.
Merzdogman, paws up, is standing (on hind legs),
violet lead loop looped over front right paw.

Intra-dialogic directions focaliser (IDF) sneezes
loudly: Staaaaaaaaaaaaa chew ???

Four Mobymarysittingwomen   (MARY BETON;
MARY SETON; MARY CARMICHAEL; ANON;
handcuffed on merzdog's violet multi-lead,
reading from open book, absorbed, audibly mumbling):
But ... But...But...
IDF: where's an extra-dialogic snot rag when you need one?

MARY BETON: Call me Mary Beton

MARY SETON: Mary Seton

MARY CARMICHAEL: Mary Carmichael

ANON: or by any name you please. We're just here as a complex set of intertexts to disrupt the convention of building a fictional past into the dramatic present.

MARY SETON: Too right. Just call us the four violations of the convention of a fixed, time-bound plane of action.

MARY BETON: Silly me! And I thought we were here to fragment fixed discursive identity and point up an alternative model of collective feminist intersubjectivity always and already in process.

MARY CARMICHAEL: OK, OK—let's just boost back to our ballad but.

Four Mobymarysittingwomen: But ... But...But...

Child: Dada!

Father: No!

Child: Dada!

Father: No!

Child: Dada!

Father: No!

Child: Dada!

Father: No!

Child: Dada! A dog is standing there!

Father: No!
Child: Dada! A dog is standing there!
Father: No!
Child: Dada! A dog is standing there!
Father: No!
Child: Dada! A dog is standing there!
Father: No!
Child: Dada! A dog is standing there!
Father: No!
Child: Dada! A dog is standing there!
Father: Where?

IDF: A small crowd gathers.

Child: Dada! A dog is standing there!
Father: No!
Child: Dada! Really, a dog is standing there!
Father: Where?

Child: Dada! A dog is standing there!
Father: What does the dog want, standing there?

Mobymarysittingwomen (handcuffed on merzdog's multi-lead, reading from open book, absorbed, audibly mumbling) turn page:
But ... But...But...

IDF: Small crowd swells.

Child: Dada! A dog is standing there!
Father: Hey, pal, a dog is standing there!
Pal: What's wrong?
Father: Hey, pal, come over hear a minute, a dog is standing here!
Pal: A dog is standing there! What does the dog want standing there? (approaching merzdog) Dog, I say, Dog what do you want standing there? Speak or move along.
Father: Save your breath, pal. Clearly this dog lacks the paralinguistic context, not to mention the basic linguistic skill set, to make your directive speech acts appear purposeful.

Child: Dada! A dog is standing there!
Father: No!
Child: Dada! A dog is standing there!
Father: No!
Child: Dada! A dog is standing there!
Father: No!
Child: Dada! A dog is standing there!
Father: What does the dog want, standing there?
IDF: Crowd growing grows restless.
Crowd: A dog is standing there! What does the dog want?

We want to know.

Father: What do you want, you dog, standing there? We want to know!

Child: Why is the dog standing there!

Crowd: A dog is standing there! What does the dog want? We want to know.

IDF: Crowd growing grows restless.

IDF: Meanwhile, Dr Michael Roger Screwtop Burke Walter Amadeus Dimble Thatch Blair Pothook is passing, with his wife Mr Melanie Dimble Pothook.

Pothook: Look, Melanie, there is a riot here.

Mr Mel D. Pothook (suddenly): What kind of a riot? Isn't it enough that I'm single-handedly opposing collusion with language as a phallogocentric sign-system? What kind of riot?

IDF: Dr Michael Roger Screwtop Burke Walter Amadeus Dimble Thatch Blair Lutetius Cameron Obadiah Osborne Pothook retorts:

Pothook: A rioting mob, of course!

Mr Mel D. Pothook (graciously, looking with his lorgnette in the direction of the mob): Michael Roger, please ask what is the matter here.

Pothook asks one of the crowd: What's happened here?

One of the crowd: A dog is standing there.

Pothook: But surely no dog is standing there.

One of the crowd: A dog is standing there.

Pothook: But why with all this mob, is a dog standing there?

One of the crowd: A dog is standing there.

Pothook: But why with all this tremendous mob, is a dog standing there?

One of the crowd: Still, in spite of this tremendous mob, a dog is standing there!

Elvis M. Stranger (in disguise): That dog is a known criminal!

IDF: A child is playing.

Child: Dada!
Father: No!
Child: Dada!
Father: No!
Child: Dada!
Father: No!
Child: Dada!
Father: No!

Child: Dada! A dog is standing there!
Father: Hey, pal, a dog is standing there!
Pal: What's wrong?
Father: Hey, pal, come over hear a minute, a dog is standing

here!

Pal: A dog is standing there! What does the dog want standing there?

Father: Well, let's all agree a dog is indeed most emphatically standing there.

IDF: Shortly afterwards Anna Nicola Fish Blossom arrives. (Anon/Anna Mhairi Nicola Fish Blossom stands up and looks every audience member in the eye)

MARY BETON: Yes, Yes, dear readers! ANNA the same ANNA from the back as from the front.

IDF: Meanwhile the crowd is humming. A low humming is humming through the crowd.

Pothook shouts: Sit! Sit!
IDF: The dog standing there stands there.

Mobysittingwomen getting louder (Anon remains standing): But ... But...

Mr Melanie D. Pothook:
Wwwwwwwwwwhhhh..........attttttttttttttt? And you want to be an independent educated dog? You cur! You dumb cur! My husband is art critic, political commentator, manager,

professor, that's manager, statesman, minister of the state of Revon, here in Revon Street in the very heart of Grubnide! You dog! You ruffian ignoramus, you dumb dunce, you benefits scrounger, you free-loading rowdy ruffian, you DOG! You—

IDF: Mr Melanie Pothook falls into a dead faint.

Elvis M. Stranger (in disguise)**:** That dog is a known criminal!

IDF (in the arms of Pothook)**:**

Mr Melanie Pothook is now in the arms of his husband, the Honorable Doctor Professor and Editor, Dr Michael Roger Screwtop Burke Walter Walter Amadeus Dimble Thatch Thatch Blair Lutetius Cameron Obadiah Osborne Pothook, Hook, Hook, Hook, Hook, Michael Roger Screwtop, Doctor Professor Editor and Manager, that's Manager of the State of Revon, here in Revon Street, in the heart of Grubnide, which means the Law, that's the Law.

Young Poet (sing-song)**:** When will you return, dear swan, my sweetheart asks for you? (Pause).

Anon:

a

mere two

of his stately plump

eight Carrara fingers
visibly from the street below milkily
he is clasping his ledger and his quill
Elvis M. Stranger marches forward, directly before the face
of the dog, and the dog is still standing.

Elvis M. Stranger (Suddenly):
Listen, People, Look at this dog, this dog challenges you.
This dog who stands here, this dog stands here, this dog
challenges you. This dog, who stands here, challenges you.
This dog, who challenges you, stands here.
This dog, who stands here, this dog stands here. This dog who
challenges you, challenges you. But that is equal to a challenge.
Or do you think that this dog is standing here
without a purpose?
Do you perhaps think this dog is standing here
for a joke?
But do you know what this dog's purpose is, the
way this dog stands here?
O you simple fools, of course, you cannot see the
fraud.
But I know this sort of dog, I know what this dog's purpose is.

This dog is an agitator, an agitator, a seducer of the people. A wrecker of civic and national security. This dog will take your job and cut open the sky. This dog will cut off your wallets and eat out the throats of your children. This dog will vomit on the foodbanks of your deserving poor. This dog will piss on your PFI, your PPI and your pie in the sky. This dog micturates on your entire Military Industrial Complex. This dog will piss on your homecoming heroes' poppies and shit on your right to one day own your own home and on your right to buy to let to buy to let to buy. This dog is no fido, no Greyfriars Bob cutened in bronze, no Scott monumental marbled Maida, but a total fiscal CU T. This dog is an agitator, an agitator, a seducer of the people.

Crowd (shout): Bravo!
Elvis M. Stranger: This dog is an agitator!
Crowd (shout): Bravo!
Elvis M. Stranger: But whoever seduces insults you.
Crowd (shout): Bravo!
Elvis M. Stranger: A people must not let itself be insulted.
Crowd (shout): Bravo!
Elvis M. Stranger: A people with honor must act.
MARY BETON (to audience): Oh, people, it's just the thugs and the scabs fooling you!
Elvis M. Stranger: The standing dog insults you! Citizens of Revon, here in the heart of Grubnide, if you have honor, act,

act, act!

Crowd (shout): Bravo!

Elvis M. Stranger: If you don't act, this dog will shame you. This standing dog has put you to shame—

IDF: At this moment the speaker is interrupted. In the sky appears a fish bearing the letters PRA, and another bearing the letters NIP.

Crowd: The author did that. It's ruined the mood.

Young Poet (stands up):

clasping his ledger and his quill, and I like to think that with these tools he is reporting to the council's equality and diversity questionnaire, while above him fall two hundred and eighty-seven steps from a height of nearly two hundred and a half feet of stony pinnacled towering edifice—

Mr Melanie Pothook (awakening and interrupting): It's time to call the police!

IDF: The Honorable Doctor Professor and Editor, Dr Michael Roger Screwtop Burke Walter Walter Amadeus Dimble Thatch Thatch Blair Lutetius Cameron Obadiah Osborne Pothook, Hook, Hook, Hook, Hook, Michael Roger Screwtop, Doctor Professor Editor, Bitter Togetherer and Manager, that's Manager of the State of Revon, Manager of the newspaper of Revon, here in the heart of Grubnide, which means the Law, that's the Law, goes personally to a few adjacent streets and looks around, until he finds a policeman who has been hiding.

The cop has the wrong idea that he is to arrest the agitator Elvis M. Stranger. But when he learns that there is only a dog at stake, who is stupidly standing, he, of course, comes along at once.

Policeman (to the dog): I regret to say I am forced to establish your identity. What's your name?
The dog stands.

IDF: This anonymous stray dog continues to violate the convention of major, named characters as a focus of interest in themselves.
The dog stands.

MARY BETON: Anna Mhairi Nicola Fish Blossom in this second lives through worlds.
(Anon becomes AMNFB, standing, looks every audience member in the eye)
Young Poet: She lives in you and in me and in many others not here tonight. She is strong. She is like a mountain. She goes on and on and—

Policeman (to the dog): I am very sorry, but I am forced to arrest you.

The dog stands.

Policeman (to the dog): A refusal would be equal to resisting authority.

The dog stands.

DF: Then something unheard-of-happens. The dog turns its head to one side.

Terror burrows into eye-lids, entrails hiss. The policeman laughs a lacquered apple. The public is tense with excitement. Everybody waits madly to know what might happen. The last of the spectators stand on their toes. A few see again the names of PRA and NIP in big first letters, coloured according to patterns.

Young Poet: A poet at bottom is something ridiculous, don't you think so? That vocation can only be excused, if one knows something. Who will be a poet in a hundred years' time?

IDF: A child is crushed between two stout crowd folk.

Child: Am I not sweet?

IDF: They throw the crushed remains of the child heedlessly under their feet. The eye sees the heaven open. A few of the smaller persons take possession of the dead child, and stand on it, because they want to see something, too.

 Mr Melanie Pothook feels painfully that he is no longer the centre of interest. Mr Melanie Pothook falls into a dead faint.

Young Poet: Do you know, ANNA, do you know it already, you can also be read from the back, and you, most magnificent one of all, you are from the back as well as in front: ANNA.

Policeman: Come along.
Policeman lifts his left leg.
The dog stands.
Policeman: Come along.
Policeman lifts his right arm, as well as his left leg.
The dog stands.
Policeman: If you don't come along, I shall have to call for reinforcements.

IDF: Now, the most unexpected thing happens. Slowly, and with the tranquillity of a perfect machine, the dog (leaving the four mobysitting women) leaves (on two legs), amiably greeting everybody, but not with the policeman, no, in an opposite direction.
The men stand silent trees.
The women shout

mobysitting women But! But! But!

IDF: The children run, shout

mobysitting women:: But! But! But!

IDF: The cop stands, like the dog before, and THE DOG LEAVES!!!!!!

IDF: Within a short time the scene of this action offers the prospect of reported future events—and distinctly the picture of a stupendous revolution. Just as the powder magazine is exploded by a spark, so will the people, as though gripped by a fearful panic run off in every direction. Tumult will whip terror into a wild flight. Some will stumble over the corpse of the crushed child, and fall down. These unfortunate ones will be dashed to pieces by the furious mob. Mr Melanie D. Pothook, reviving from his most recent dead faint, will receive on this occasion the blow of a boot in the region of his abdomen, and will fall into one more fainting fit. And one, two, three, four, five persons will remain behind, not counting the dead bodies.

The cop, too, will remain standing and writes down the facts, one of the chief tasks of the local police. He notes down, that an unidentified dog, who will remain also unknown to those present, is responsible as a result of its illegal behaviour, for the death of one, two, three, four, five persons and a child of the city of Grubnide, in the Free State of Revon. Consequently the cop finds himself obliged, though with regret, to arrest the dog in time. But to his regret the dog has escaped arrest by such a rapid flight that, to his great regret, this flight could not have been prevented, especially since the police at this time and this place do not consist of adequate forces.

Policeman: I do want to apologise to the people of Grubnide. I do also want to be part of the solution. I am truly sorry for the loss. I am also sorry it is taking so long to remove the dead from the street.

Young Poet: The days of the small separate statue are over, well over, but even so—

IDF: To his regret, or rather as a result, however, there have and will have occurred a few regrettable accidents, and now follows their enumeration. The remaining spectators are noted down as witnesses. Elvis M. Stranger gives his name on this occasion as Dandie Dinmont.

Elvis M. Stranger: My name is Dandie Dinmont.

IDF: Then follows the official seizure of the dead bodies. They will be stamped, weighed, examined for trichinas (FYI that's worms!), or taken to the morgue for the establishment of their identities, one of the chief tasks of the local police.

A huge elephant, however, will run with an electric bell through Revon Street, in Grubnide, in Revon, violating the plot structure and cry: Extraordinary session of Parliament, extraordinary session of Parliament; the question at stake is nothing less than the outbreak of the great and glorious revolution in Revon Street, in the city of Grubnide, in Revon.

Young Poet: (closing song) [LOOKING AT AUDIENCE]: and one such Dandie Dinmont will one day help 'Burke, Sir Walter' to count beyond the two fat fingers that are currently all he needs to log the total number of individual public statues erected in this city of Grubnide to commemorate a lived historical woman—of which there are two: [COUNT ON FINGERS] 1. Empress Queen Victoria, that sometime satirically saltired pigeon-cosher, who corks the foot of Leith Walk; 2. humble Helen Crummy, who heroically rouses all Craigmillar to music on Niddrie Mains Road. Both women outnumbered and outflanked by three city-centred mutts: [COUNT ON FINGERS] 1. old Walter Scott's marbled Maida is the ruling paw of Princes Street, East; 2. Greyfriars Bobby, the Old Town's bronzed faithful, is the sweetly cheesing corner star of Candlemaker Row; 3. while Princes Street, West, is turf now to Greyfriars Bobby's San Diego prone bronze twin, a great new subaltern lump—a—dog—called—'Bum'.
Seriously???!!

SEKXPHRASTIKS: RITZFROLIKS

There is material to be seen around you everyday. But one day something—some one thing—pops out at you, and you pick it up, and you take it over, and you put it somewhere else, and it fits, it's just the right thing at the right moment. You can do the same thing with words or with metal.

—**John Chamberlain**

BLUE BROWNIES EAT LEMONS

sea blued
a tertiary
yellowgreen

yellows
frosting
a tertiary

bluegreen
into this
trembling

neutrality
a blue while
is caressing

a creamed grey
it beiges
to deflect

a low white
flash into
a blue nether

hardly
touching
themselves

at all
blue brownies
radiate red

IN THE GARDENS
WITH JOHNNY WOOLSTANZA

outside the house is tuning
the pond is being prepared
art inside is always unlabeled

the pond is being prepared
outside the trees are ticketed
for the return of reg's girl

she will be moved closer
to the centre of the pond
will there be carp and water-lily?

johnny uncorks the lawn
where henry's bronzes
used to yawn

RITZFROLIC

let's just wait here at the rope
look i-i'm touching the pale green
there's a blue child

i-i understand but i-i don't care
let's pull up the peg
watch the instant circus

WISHINGWELLWINK

last pink one
behind you
i-i like that hydrangea

stay for a photo
it's called
wishing something

NAUGHTYNIGHTCAP

it's the kind of place
it changes
arthur don't touch

i-i have that in my garden
presente la vernabula
this one is pink

FIDDLERSFORTUNE

smile but no hello
a lot of that stuff going on
do we go through there?

i-i understand but i-i don't care
it doesn't smell like grass
                    i-i'm going to try not to lose you

GONDOLA GONDOLA WALT WHITMAN
OUT OF JOHNNY'S GONDOLA
ENDLESSY—

something upward libid prongs

night long on the prong

the long stretch island

worn poet: fever rebel

so quiet island lips

mad for the hook

leave little wrecks on fish island

urge and spur every life

discover the urge of mistake

INFOPO (GONDOLA GONDOLA:
WORDS ON WORDS)

a poet might arrange the language of information
as a sculptor arranges motorcar parts
applying paint to the already painted
choosing a word—or two or three words
because of what they look like in print
and when they look good together in print
and they're having a good time together
no-one expects to drive off the garage
forecourt in what results in hope of shops
or bank or job and neither object is a flat-pack
for anything else (neither object *is* anything else
but itself) for there is nothing to decode here
and no-one has yet disproved karl kraus's
theory of general creativity which posits
the beyond help of literature in its material
ground in the language of information nor
his forecast that a prohibition on all language
of information would not prevent the people
quickly learning 'to answer the aria "how's
        business?"
with a still life' therefore caveat: where once
were bent fenders or a painted chassis now are

new art supplies in whatever lies here and in
        colour
in forms in rhythms in spaces in numbers
(in reverence for nines and fours and square
roots) that embrace or collide dis-
solve re-form travel in fit in form
in colour (squeeze wad melt) but still they are
bent fenders or a painted chassis and yet there is
        music
in a daily car ride some necessary common
ground and yes so much depends
upon an arrangement of bent fenders
glazed by spray-paint beside the red chassis
that i will tell you for free the following nine
things (they will not get you to work
on time) about a decorum in car
parts and a welding of fenders i-i bent earlier
a few hand-painted spray-painted chassis:

      1. John Chamberlain dedicated *Luna, Luna,*
Luna (1970) [25. UPSTAIRS ROOM] to
Elaine Chamberlain (his second wife) in 1979, six
years after her death in 1973. A life long lover of
nines and square roots, John Chamberlain married
Prudence Fairweather (his fourth wife) twice in
1996: on 9th June and 6th September.

      2. Kurt Merz Schwitters, the 20th

century's greatest assemblage artist and poet, was an acknowledged inspiration to John Chamberlain. Kurt Merz Schwitters spent his final years in poverty and obscurity on a farm in the English lake district where he died in 1948.

3. The poet Sylvia Plath was also a collagist. The London flat in which she killed herself was once occupied by the poet W.B. Yeats.

4. *Toasted Hitlers* (1977) is a painted and chromium-plated car-part assemblage by John Chamberlain not in the present exhibition. I-i wish it were! It is an excellent counter work to *Luna, Luna, Luna*, which is.

5. In the summer of 1981, John Chamberlain exhibited car-part assemblages *Essex* (1960) and *Exciter* [aka *White Shadow*] (1962) and the giant foam sofa, *American Barge* (1979), in the huge survey exhibition, *Westkunst*, in Köln [Cologne], Germany. I-i attended *Westkunst* with my father in the July of 1981—a formative experience.

6. In the same summer (June 1981) my 21st birthday party was held on a barge going down Doncaster canal.

7. A year later, in 1982, my father attended and reported back on d7: documenta 7, the 7th of a series of 100-day exhibitions of 1000 works of modern art held every 5 years in Kassel, Germany. documenta 1 was held in 1955. At d7 in 1982 the first oak was planted of Joseph Beuy's *seven thousand oaks*. Also shown were two gondolas by John Chamberlain.

8. Michael Heseltine served as Secretary of State for the Environment 1979-1983 in the first term of the Tory government led by Margaret Hilda Thatcher.

9. Margaret Hilda Thatcher died 8th April 2013. Nine days later, in accordance with her wishes, she received a ceremonial funeral with full military honours.

MERZFIT FOR JOHNNY WOOLSTANZA
LADY LAZARUS HAS WHEELS

You should have known
the rough beast
would make you
turn on the gas;

and answered the ad
of an Anna Blume
(Cylinders Farm
is crowless:

no kunst
to bother you,
but a barn
full of Merz).

Turn blue spokes
red, go Deutsch
shelling yellow
phonemes

into the dusk.
What say the people?
Lady Lazarus
has wheels!

JOHNNY I-I HARDLY KNEW

^

in eighty-one all
at sixes in köln's
westkunst just
twenty-one so
excited by your
exciter-motor

i-i creamed red

a mere gull
a rude girl
spiked green
back-comb plated
lime-streaked locks
red-lipped red

essexed in black
gold too a fine
fit for your
custom-painted
chromium-plated
steel deco essex
my exact vintage

i-i not long off
a wet birthday
barge that cut
doomtown canal (d.
o. b. seven six
nineteen sixty)
in a three
seven
clash

with pa it's true
i-i grat foam
born at the door
of your american
barge settee

<elbows out>

make
way
for
yes
another
barge
party

^ ^

in eighty-two all at
sixes at the seventh d
is beuy's first oak
planted at the castle
ripping right past his seven
thousand basalts wedged

(one big caspar against time)

at the front door is pa
merely one of three
hundred and eighty-seven
thousand three hundred and
eighty-one visitors
i-i know he saw all one

thousand exhibits by one

hundred and eighty-
two artists including you
johnny including you

but was he really
looking johnny did he

really see the gondola
denton or the gondola
theodosia

(gondola denton
already ripe with
condolences for hart
crane gondola
theodosia
in beetle for marianne
moore) for johnny

i-i hardly knew black
mountain back then you
taught me hart crane
you brought to me
marianne moore
in her own truck
what the fuck i-i
felt it all—all of it
was free—for johnny

i-i hardly knew (until
i-i googled) the d seven
budget was six million
nine hundred and fifty-

seven thousand nine
hundred and seventy-
seven deutsche mark
(or in euros three million
five hundred and fifty-seven
thousand five hundred
and fifty-five) but who
the catullus is counting?

michael
heseltine
busy
it seems
planting
trees in
toxteth

you called it
johnny: *it*
ain't cheap

LEGEND HAS IT
(HILDAFIT FOR *TOASTED HITLERS*)

a phial of less well burnt bone
fragments and blood-dimmed carpet

fibres taken from the torn bodies
charcoaled in the cratered garden

of the chancellery eventually
fell to the hands of a young

undergraduate in chemistry
at somerville college oxford

researching bactericidal
gramicidin (an early topical

antibiotic culture
allowing inorganic

malevolent monovalent
cations unrestricted travel

through cellular membranes)

which very suspension—*contra* all

medical wisdom of the time *re*
gramicidin (external use

only) and of much later *re*
the high temperature levels

required in rendering offal
and bone meal safe from that

epizootic new variant
Creutzfeldt–Jakob—once ingested

formed the foul catalyst by
which is now afforded what

history so valiantly denied
a full state funeral the full

global artilleried glory
of these gun carriage

military honours for
the führer dead and his new bride

HALOFIT: *LUNA LUNA LUNA*

consider its optical depth this
mineral-coated synthetic polymer
resin smudged by the artist's own

fingers his universe has been caught
here in its own gravitational lens
radiating hot lemon into fuscia pink

pulsing to blue-green electric pelt
you don't have to be a professor of
quantitative cosmology specializing in high

redshift galaxies operating a galaxy
and mass assembly panchromatic
swarp imager to see at large distances

into the past high peaks in the cosmic
density field or understand the statistical
data of cosmological density maxima

(with peacock and heavens) or surpass
that past-oriented peak model to
appreciate present-day clustering

with the new halofit model or to check
out 2dFGRS Xi active gif along
with 2dFGRS Xi passive gif (at

six vee dot-row dot-hack dot new-key
four word slash tilde chap) where
to this rudely untutored eye the universe

is clearly an exquisitely iridescent lusciously
living cunt—no you do not need halofit to see
all of it expand in the fixed polymer loss of her

his love: LUNA LUNA LUNA

SEKXPHRASTIKS: FIZZ

WE WORE (RED)

lipstick (drop-dead) avec pendant cigarette;
diamanted, gin-martinied (olive-stillhettoed)—all
high-stem gilded; lush black fan-tailed
frocks, all cocktailed, jet-beaded, backlessed;
exhumed refuge, slash-sleeved, plunged
taffeta, drop-weighted at the hem; skirts fad-
ed, gold-spun, bias cut
found our fragment selves (collect-
ing here, now) lit red, showered lavender,
twisting in the twisting electric vector
our mirror ball lifting the Miro in us all,
our universal Picasso, our luminous piss-
translucent walls aglow with the barely known
mothers of us all (WoolfenStein)

and Money's Too Tight (To Mention)
belts out—Valentine Brothers—and
lovers in the next room play Fever
at thirty-three revolutions per minute,
then 78,
spread rain-stained coats, red-lined.

Out-stretched arms, up-raised hands
cut at the cruel night—
jive-signing the peace.
Stand Down Margaret warred with Mack
the Knife—torn fish-netted scar-
lets kicked like sharks, birled in D
Ms (de rigeur); rude stars studded,
sickle moons embossed limp lapels
(enfolding black halter-necked crepe);
powder pinked cowboys tracked cactus across
shirt collars, rode high as if what we wore—dis-
avowing metaphor, worn dishabille,
the dead's fretted retros—rode us.

SIMILE

is as if we can see all the stitches
at the seams of the borrowed dress you
wear to the Wee Red Bar, your flat-mate
next night to a Fire Engines gig—on whose hips it

falls a bit differently (for you it's all throat);
but there's no stitch to see *au pays*
de metaphor, where the frock heads off
(without so much as an as if) *toute*

seule to the Hoochie Coochie Club; and girls
of slender means, we meet the peachy dawn,
fingering golden cinches, our diamante clasps,
all blurry-eyes, suspiring: *who is she*

walking home now? We long to press back
the fine wool crepe, to take a damp cloth
to crushed pleats, to pin the torn hem, suspend
in wilful lavender, hope against stains.

CAROLINE'S DRESSES

Arrived east from the Borders
with cable-knit sweaters and soft
woollen plaid skirts: herring-bone
tweed, tailored and lined, formal
school pinafores, and the sweetest
daisy frock for birthday parties
in yellow-flecked white broidery
anglaise with silken pink sash
(How I grat at the loss of it
posted back west for Julia's turn)

Hung forlorn and so empty, those
treacly black bouclés, fur trimmed,
the thinned pink or teale silks,
swaying on the wire hangers still
hooked to the back of doors
in the silent flat in Tarvit
Street (you'd just left for New York
then the lone turret in Marchmont)

Partied hardest and wild, all cross
cut, bias jived and birling, burst
from the huge three door armoire

at the height of Huntly Street:
the classic black-and-white chequered
summer frock full-pleated twin
to the one striped in the colours
of Klee that bled at the hem
in some Mediterranean
shallows; the dove grey suit, plunged
felt-faced lapels and nipped waist,
brooched with gold and pearls, or pinned
by soft amethysts; and the two
most favoured of evening noirs:
that sleek bias-cut gown
with fret-worked slashed sleeves,
and slash neck set off by a white
cord of white Venetian beads low
knotted at the belly where
the stitched deco angles meet
in geometric over-seamed
panels down to the ankles;
and that inky cocktail crepe
with that inky satin bow
at the high throat and the spine
of inky covered buttons—
These were the raiments, the very
commonwealth of thrilling glamour

(Are they not now all just sulking
in their misty camphor, retired
to the back of the closet in your quiet
border cottage—now that all we ever
seem to wear ends in trousers?)

HERE COME HUGE TEARS

i-i don't like dull narcotics so
it's once more for forced fingers, mouthy blinds,
rude fragments, so light the neon spheres of
OPEN, let slide the phosphor-
escent Lenin, turn up the trouvé tapestry
Elvis in black cross-stitched silhouette,
raise high the deep blue martini glasses
and load the blue guitar;
roll out the diamanté clips—
here come huge tears
for Caroline
(Ca)

wear them in the silenced streets
glaze in stars smudging cheeks
drown salty talk at the very lip
let them shine up disquietude until it blazes
wet beaded sparks (let be be its own finale and
        seem
to its own devices) i-i have dipped these words
in huge—

her brush has dipped wild unrest
her change of touch has nursed the lark deep
into the solid Border hills: the wall opens out
all its glory enamelled in sleek opacity
black shimmers viscid blue already snakes
fast into canvas striding truly out as the waves
greet us with *pour quoi pas* nowhere else to go
but gathering just here at the first touched
        glimmer
of lemon (at the twinkle of pink) green gold
        glisten
blue lines shear moist air
fine cross-hairs float violet here
the lush blue interior of these our möbius selves
shaping ourselves shaping our worlds
as we go

BORDER THOUGHTS (IBIZA)

Caroline is dead; Ca is fizz
out of ventricles. Who will paint

the Selgovae and the Romans
for the Palestinians now? Her

border thoughts follow me to blue
Spain where blue towels stripe the white

plastic slatted chair and the frosted
screen sorrows a clearing sky

vapours score silver into pale
blue cloud cranes idle over

the prison out there they are slowly
making an hotel citadel

rosied fingers over the rock
a mere towel slung on the gold

balcony rail holds up the bay (far
off the pharos dark-tipped). Velvet

laps at the glass the island
glade bobs to the horizon

baffles the gold frame the bird-
skimmed sea refuses to glaze

the sun refuses the cloud right
into the pink as the plane climbs

en plein air the towels are bone
dried to the white plastic slats.

Under this hand the blue pilot
pen presses to the paper's edge

(stationery of the hotel Torre)
where Ca is fizz displaced;

Caroline the sun goes lemon
the water stripes a shaky gold

a boat slides over the rail
pulls the sea gold above it

singular mast the one vertical
spindle glides tuning across

a ribbon now of black islands
up pushing green over the bar

in this beautiful shuttle of light
drifts the gentlest of currents

BORDER THOUGHTS
(TRAQUAIR STUDIO)

lightly held in absence
gleaned in bold woods burnt mounds
her beacon fires smoulder
shelved cordons of THIS IS
MICROWAVE OVEN SAFE semi-
transparent plastic lidded
cheesewells of sorts coot
stones handfasted waulked
in minchmoor to the pure
and cold her powerhouse
shears into the law she mills
burns seals into the strange
lands all of these she has
combed from the bold rigs
i-i hold now these four

∧

decapitated clay
pipe stems all shattered
a grimy shank length chased

with W.CHAS all
a-tinkle one thumb size
pipe bowl (intact) at odds
with two incompatible
demi-spherical lung
lobes the chipped one mono
grammed T.W.
the other something T.
three palm smoothed clay
balls (a plunker, a pattie,
a peasie) click and roll

∧ ∧

doll's head early plastic
size of a child's fist
shut-eyed plastic skull
cracked at the mold's seam
plastic plastic plastic
clown's head on screw stump
plastic plastic plastic
potted fern its root exposed
plastic plastic plastic
yellowed peeling tiny
wind-up steam engine

blue firebox blue coupling
red smokestack red wheels
plastic plastic plastic
shard of santa hat
plastic plastic plastic
an opalescent sew-through
blouse button two holed
shoogles a loose 100
lire coin brightly stamped
Republica Italiana
1978

^ ^ ^

crenellated bottlecap stamped
            sC Ws
stem windered steel watch-rim
bent-lipped STAINLESS CHROME-PLATE
SHEFFIELD soup spoon nicely
level still in handle
a corroded wire ruff
of pitted plumbago
a corroded coat hook
a spindled plate switch disk
arrowed FAST to SLOW

fork prongs corroded in ∏
rust ringed by the lost
shaft collar a button cap
an oval tab a steel chain
bracelet quite untarnished
pulley wheels once white
two belt clasps one stamped
by an orphaned M & Co
bent lightly to meet the other's
gate stamped PARIS
and SOLIDE below
a galvanized clamp
three loops of barbed
wire a crotchet shorn
from metal facing
the emptied churn
of a .22 rifle
cartridge its round end SHAKE
BEFORE/ USE / THIS END
UP noses the exposed
interior flank of the fixed
tin bullet chamber torn
caramelized from a die
cast wild west cap gun

^ ^ ^ ^

shards of jug handles
curving arcs of cup ligaments
loop simples and rests
broken square-brokens white
porcelain and cream slip
ware one foot shard in blue
broken letter-stems cup
commas glazed descenders
brittle bowls snapped
ascenders and sharp bars
arabesques in *c* and *r*
one last faience still ringed
to its shard of cup wall
i-i want it for an *a*
or a dunted piece of *o*
to raster the long ridge
a sintered line a broken serif
a kerning held for Ca

ARCHIE CALLING: ALTAFORTE!

'Hello J., Archie here' would strike a peace
of sorts. 'Three new ones for you'—pure music.
Damn Priest (Hoovering) left out to clash
with Priest (Ironing). We halt opposite
fresh judiciary. All three march crimson
off Isa's bedroom wall. Is she happy?

Ay, sleeps all night under them, quite happy.
His Priest (Hoovering) would strike a peace
in Hell. 'They Three Judges took all my crimson'
he fumes. Finding the next takes music.
We shove Muirhouse Ox to the wall opposite,
and wait while, stirrer, he sticks on The Clash.

Mythical Muirhouse Ox probably did clash
once with yon Headless Pilton Dog. Happy
hangs Brixton Academy. Opposite:
brazen boots and bronze jacket struck in peace.
Next, Joseph Beuys (portrait). Next, pure music!
His Crematorium once flamed crimson,

gold, blues—til it bled all its crimson
'to varnished scabs', he mourns. How could they clash
against this ineradicable red music?
These pure rogue pigments replicate: Happy
Warriston Crematorium! Let peace
combust too in this ghost copse opposite

Ward One, the Royal Ed. Opposite,
the venereal clinic curds its crimson
peaks in a concupiscent peace.
His vista north from Drylaw does clash
since the gasometer got blown, unhappy
postscript in blue belated blade music.

In the jive of his palette knife, a music
of impossible impasto rises. Opposite,
a blue disappointed Brighton Pier is happi-
ness. All his blues now whip to crimson.
Where his black waves battle, lush hues clash:
weltering web. Ay, Archie's call strikes peace

of sorts. Chuck Art School in the dock, greet crimson.
Hell makes music in Drylaw: two sevens clash.
Hell blot black Archie's video box 'at peace'!

BROOMHILL

blue garden
still ripples
fresh on canvas

cool garden
tremors blossom
fizz on canvas

fruit garden
stark shimmers
fuse on canvas

studio garden
scent flickers
fast on canvas

A JULIA SKY

Today's is a Julia sky
low and late light sears
into chimneys sweetly butters
the number five speed sign
on the side gates to the brewery

now ports in the chalky air
pinkened they still deliver
up from sharp edged shadows
through cream tinctured sorrows
to the cool curving rooves

a glisten where the wet slates
are about to blossom
in a generosity of blue
because today Julia's sky
declares itself open

WATCHING SHARLEEN PLAY (VIOLIN)

Slides mere horse-hair, tight
on pernambuco, pure
over pulsing gut, and her
figuring fingers release

a thousand true arrows
into blue keening air.
Shimmering sisters we dare
hardly breathe as we hold

our daughters, watch them watch
Sharleen play, see her hold
herself to the perfect yet
changing form of the notes,

shift the music's shapes
in the soft moon shafts
of sonata, or, high
on Debussy or Haydn, she

sets loose complexity,
limbers to crescendo,
cuts the maiden to quartzy

ice flung, unyielding, against

this death—plucks the bleak jig
of Schubert into the brink
of a Stravinsky spring.
We watch her figuring fingers

coax sheer joy sul ponti-
cello. She reaps us all
to raptures in the slip
of her glissando.

FLYING COLIN HERD

i-i have just read click + collect
non-stop
on a cross channel flight i-i was in c
d g before i-i knew it the first click
is the deepest
herding of the soon to be dead
over the bleak monitor
in the opening pages
or the black square
saying stop yes we could stop
(all this surfacing) if we put our thumbs
down + then it's really just a case
of having truly noticed some of the very
worst that the world has been doing +
still does do to being all too soon
on a trip to collect what we can
that is good or we need to think
about more or just really look at for a
while + listen too to a sparrow or a
sparrow + a sporran
i-i'm not saying
it's all hot scoop + easy jet
for the entire read just that when

the woman in the seat in front acting all
air traffic control mum on a mission
to explain to her kids pointed out
the eiffel tower as we were coming in
to land + then actual concorde on the tarmac
outside + another woman with a torn
face + mickey ears with matching child
+ mickey ears queuing for the toilet
looked about to go into a crazy sulk
+ maybe to start up a kerfuffle
with the stewardess i-i didn't even
look up i-i couldn't stop reading click
+ collect i-i couldn't stop
clicking + collecting even when i-i got
to the frog on the last page i-i was looking
back at the lily pad for more more more
encore encore colin i-i said encore not even
noticing security checking my passport or how
quickly i-i was getting my bag off
the carousel (i-i know) to head out now
on grandes lignes for the tgv
south into a sunlight
+ feeling so brand new

CODA

+ now colin herd
has given the red
ceilings his swamp
kiss yes swamp kiss
it sucks everything in
everything—it's
a scandal broth
of bath mat +
sunken butt
swipe colin herd
click + collect

CODA CODA

+ now colin herd
has made you name it
for dostoevsky wannabe
yes go ahead you name it
+ you will find it
in you name it by colin herd
even i-i'm in it we are all
of us in it invited to name it
the title is you name it

this foaming discursive space
you name it + out
out it comes excessively
spun very hot + wet
+ totally gross not gross
in a prince andrew way
but gross in a good way
in an elizabeth grosz
way somatic all fluctuating
social + fluid + living
+ sexual + cultural
encoded possibilities
+ a queer foamy polity
that saves us from wading
through peter sloterdijk's
spherology in all its
thick description of the forms
of human inhabitation in all
their foamy material
+ semantic specificity
(even his editor says
the problem with sloterdijk
is that you are always eight
thousand pages behind)
+ utterly embarrassing
you name it is embarrassing

in a good way in a colin
herd way yes you name it
is a foaming triumph
of fancy surfacing surfaces
fancyifying surfacing
finally this is the surfeit
of surface the foamy meniscus
where all our bubbles rise
did i-i just say finally?
finally this is the surfeit
of surface the foamy meniscus
where all our bubbles rise
if poetry is champagne
(what else could it be but
language in malolactic
fermentation) + everything
that is flying everything
that is groaning everything
that is rolling everything
that is singing everything
that is speaking everything
that is rising everything
that converges everything
that is bubbling is saying
yes the wind the wave the star
the bird the clock the bubble

everything that these bubbles say
yes if poetry is champagne
(these bubbles rise to say)
then you name
it by colin herd
is grand cuvée
yes colin herd
is grand cuvée
enivrez-vous
enivrez-vous sans cesse

LILA MATSUMOTO

any minute now
with urn & drum
lila matsumoto
will crest the hill
queen of scree
queen of pip
kitchen allegorist
queen of all kitchen
sinking tapas parties
she has reached
into boxy
to find soxy
she has tossed us
her soft troika
blazing queen
among
the heather
slip-streaming
sound-tracking
lila matsumoto
her différance
is spreading

ORISON TO IAIN MORRISON

i-i'm on a i-i'm in a i-i'm at an horizon of an orison
        by iain morrison
i-i'm a i'm i'm a iain morrison a iain morrison
        daughter
        i-i mean to say
i-i'm on a i-i'm in a i-i'm at an horizon of an
        orison an
        orison to iain morrison

i-i mean to say i-i'm on edge reading iain at
        an horizon
in an orison by iain morrison
iain morrison i-i mean to say his work your
        work i-i'm
        i-i'm a huge fan huge a huge fan
of his work of his pretty circles of your
        pretty circles
they carry me your circles carry

iain morrison i-i want to say you can dismiss
      me i-i
      mean it dismiss me any time i-i'm
going to dim it now dim it mid spin mid eddy mid
      sunder an orison a daughter an iain
morrison orison to iain morrison i-i want to say
      ask may
i-i be a daughter a daughter of sorts?

HOW YOUR BONE-WHITE PIPS ALICE

fall douce soft on hard solstice
sting plunk from a ripe sky
i-i deep in some word caves
minding gaps for breath space
into a stillness of the small hours
seeking unique signs of universal play
i-i am listening for the sweet rasp
of a language that is free and honest
made by someone being free and honest

how even the year's shortest day
cannot hold off the last spasm
how a news announced at six
at ten at midnight still chimes
its bogus phatic communion
with big ben how a legal time
is still said by a man with a bbc accent
follows five short pips then a long one:
bip–bip–bip–bip–bip—*beep*
how your bone-white pips say:
my name is tom—is not dead

OOR MOBY: MÖBIUS
    (or swipe up from the bottom bezel)

    GEO
    SULLY
    SUB
    STANCE

    GEO
    SULLY
    SUB
    STANCE

            here her
            diamante

            scatters

            stop lights
            drops red

    a green coign
    a green coign
    of vantage

                                        at vet

                                        corner

          GEO
          SULLY
          SUB
          STANCE

          GEO
          SULLY
          SUB
          STANCE

outside
          vivi
                secting

a room

          GEO
          SULLY
          SUB
          STANCE

GEO
SULLY
SUB
STANCE

who decided to archive the perimeter fence?

unhinge all the doors; swallow your key

on exit (in case of dry ice alarm)

try jawbone walk
at middle meadow
in light ruined moonlight
sans teeth sans jaw
without a whale

> or bring some knitting
> and a ball

    this is

OOR MOBY
OORURMOBY
OORA'BODY's MOBY
MÖBIUS

MOBYMÖBIUS

MOBY(   )VET

MOBYMERZ

MOBYPIN

MOBYDADA

MOBYMAMA

MOBYBECHET

MOBYBESSIE

MOBYMELLY

MOBYSTEIN

MOBYWOOLFENSTEIN MOBYWEINSTEIN

MOBYWEST

MOBYMUIR

MOBYPULPY

MOBYAMPERSAND

MOBY&

MOBYPULPY&

MOBYSTAIN

MOBYFIN

MOBYFINFAROUT

MOBYFENÊTRE

MOBYWINDOWPEEL

MOBYSUGARDOCKS

MOBYHOWL

MOBYWRECK

MOBYVRBA

MOBYNINA
MOBYNANA
MOBYMODOTTI
MOBYPHALLE
MOBYPISSFACTORY
MOBYPIPPILOTTI
MOBY291
MOBY369
MOBYWEEREDBAR

MOBYOUTSIDE(THE NARRATIVE)
MOBYUNDIGEST
MOBYCU T

MOBYCCA
MOBYIVY
MOBYVERSEHEARSE
MOBYSUTTON
MOBY10RED
MOBYVESPERS
MOBYCAESURA
MOBYSHAKESPEARE&CO
MOBYSPL
MOBYEMBASSY

MOBYLIGHTHOUSE
MOBYPOETRYCLUB
MOBYNGS
MOBYCOOPER
MOBYFRUITMARKET
MOBYCAMPLELINE

MOBYPIP
MOBY12
MOBYMOON
MOBYMAYBE

MOBYGEO
MOBYGEOSULLY
MOBYGEOSULLYSUBSTANCE

MOBY
GEO
SULLY
SUB
STANCE

MOBYMÖBIUS
or:

1. Swipe up from the bottom bezel of your iPhone to bring up Control Center.

2. Tap the Flashlight button at the bottom left.

3. Point the LED flash on the back of your iPhone at whatever you want to light up.

SO LOVE YOU WHEN

the bealach glistens
you drop to cup
glimmering spawn
from hot tarmac
into the cool, wet burn.

SEKXPHRASTIKS: TUTELAGE

TRIPTYCH

∧

Fifty minutes to break.

My body, like the building, talks
to me in twinges, takes
twenty minutes to numb pressure
points. My foot is my clock.

Days dissected by silent weight
invisibly shifting,
parcels of hip-strain and knee-
lock.

Standing flesh weeps;
grinds from stasis a sweat.

Trickles chance from lip, pit, breast.

Hot springs cool along my spine.

∧ ∧

Naked and nothing i-i live an hour
in my ribs and right thigh. I-i stand hip-

locked come break time, mustn't move from here
before the chalking of the feet to the floor

anchors empty columns pinning air
down to ghost portals i-i'll fall into ten

minutes later.
              Shove out an old wall
for the feel of that catch in that hip

flex a blade then settle the ribs and load
my thigh. Naked i-i place my jar

∧ ∧ ∧

a space to think in naked
anchored to the hourly rate

drift in absent taxi (space, heat, light)

no it's not for the simulacra of has been
not the endlessness of vain

but a space we forge here in studio

is why the figurative is
for the model (always abstract)

WAYS OF SEEING

ECA ECA ECA

a nude is never alone

the studio bristles to my lip

D&P D&P D&P

south of the esplanade

across the wind well

ECA ECA ECA

flotsam high on electric

heat beached on charcoal

ECA D&P ECA

look north to the rocky home

to the city's dreaming fist

D&P D&P D&P

there on the esplanade burnt

burnt alive burnt to charcoal

THESE LEGS

These legs. Prisons for pride.
These legs on which standing nudes
stand.

REST ROOM

                  Surplus poseuses
remembering mouths how to use them
first to drag a cigarette and list
the pains and thousand stupidities tedium
fingered

                  Rub your arse for home
stretch one more fag then limp back late, fuck
the moaning cunt who got away early
while your tyro princess rips to a new sheet
with ten last fucking standing minutes to go

DRAPE

One evening i-i sat for head life
with a secret Nazi
on drape in the next class

i-i came for him at half-time
dead curious, and found
his scattered half-portrait

empty, half-hanging from brushes,
ground almost
to naked eyes.

UNSEATED

a plastered throne slid
its perfectly solid embrace

on stolen hospitality ("Don't
sit on it silly. Just look!")

has sloughed fine trails of white
magic on the silk black fanned

train of my borrowed cocktail
dress swagged like the curtains

welcome to gate-crash
streaming wildest ormolu

i-i woke alone on the bed
winks at me now white

and unsat-in since you say
from quiet corners

RECLINING

Think of this body as a landscape.
Let it lie flat in its crests and

valleys across your long horizon.
Don't try to pick it up with your paint

brush. Explore
                these your new distances.

Above all, you must make it lie down.

SEATED

Legs then bigger
out toward you
knees higher
buttocks back
massive
make the torso
sit solid show
the build of the neck
on which to found
the chin up head.

Hands rest
heavy enlarge
over knees
shinning out
enlarge load-
bearing easy feet
bang against foreshortened
legs and distant solar plexus vista.

STANDING

You must follow
the twisting lines
of contrap-
            posto
head to hip

mid-twist
is the torso.

Follow the breast
of jut and turn
entwining drape.

An elbow raised
to cradle head,
open fingers
linger on a lost
shoulder
fallen yes
in contrap-
            posto.

(Locked knee
solid foot
brace hard
below.)

WALKING

mark the gesture
tilt of head
fall of hand
wheel of knee
sweep of foot
chalk in flow
arm to paper

INTERIOR

Make this figure
punctuate
architecture's smile.
Build it to the table,
the seat, and mirror.
All that it breaks
ceiling, wall, floor
must converge.

HEAD LIFE

Circle the cranium
from your shoulder.
Build into the sphere
without choice
of her features
your face.

LAUGH WHEN THEY TELL YOU HOW

the pose they set left the model's arse
tartan, as if they could make marks
that last, as if they were marking us

MR EDUARDO

stood with family for the standard
life portico he can stand all day

all week contrapposto he says
stretch take fruit for your lunch

water at every break and remember
the first five years are the hardest

AFTER LIFE

Yes, you can always tell a model by,
it is said, a sort of patina
when they settle

THE PLEASURES OF MY BODY

standing kneeling seated reclining draped nude
never naked always silent
        i-i watch i-i watched
one photographer
attempt and fail
to shoot me naked
i-i shot him right back

in woods near the village
he asked if i-i would mind
if he photographed
between my legs

not necessarily
i-i said thinking
of greer in suck
but to consent

I-I LOVE MY BODY

i-i would want i-i said
some good reason
why he wanted

to put his camera

into my cunt
he had no reason
that met my consent
therefore he did not

put his camera
into my cunt
to my surprise
he consented

to supplying
a photograph
of his priapic
dick to collage

onto a clipped
newspaper image
of the prime
minister it was
1979
ejaculating
a strapline for
a stronger pound

not exactly
heartfield
not exactly
magritte ceci
n'est pas une
pipe the word

dog does not bark
the photographed
cock
does not stand
does not cum

the phallus
is not
the penis
this is
the treachery
of gender
gender is
a metaphor

it is
2017
the world
is gone

digital
another
patriarchal
woman may be
prime minister
so what?

    NOT EVERY MAN HAS A PENIS
    NOT EVERY WOMAN HAS A VAGINA
    NOT EVERY PATRIARCH IS A MAN
    NOT EVERY MAN A PATRIARCH
    NOT EVERY WOMAN IS A FEMINIST
    NOT EVERY FEMINIST A WOMAN

BINARY [CONTAINS]

              QUEER OVER

                      FLOWS

EVERY HUMAN AN ANIMAL
EVERY HUMAN AN INSTANCE

A UNIQUE
INSTANCE

OF A UNIVERSAL

(DIVERSELY
EMBODIED)

SUB/JECT

I-I LOVE MY BODY

THE PLEASURES

OF MY BODY

SEKXPHRASTIKS: NONAGE

CHILDREN OF THE ARTIST

in hats
Post Office peaked
and Dutch straw
under which we sat
all ears but mouthless

and in another—
except for me—
no eyes even
naked too.

Group portraits
did not last.

Singled out
picked off
in pencil studies
as likely

dropped
for abstracts
nudes in landscapes

or re-arranged

in a montage
of family snaps.

THE ARTIST

makes colours
sing on paper
lines of pleasure.

The self-portrait, however,
is an acquired taste.

PHOTOGRAPH

Sun from the sea would set
somewhere behind the farm.
Backs to our blushing waves
and the narrow strip between
we basked for his blackened camera.

Tender tots in silence rub arms
squint fat sets of oceanic
cheeks, immobile for now
but beginning to furrow
into faces we recognise.

SOMETIMES

there's just rain and the mirror
won't light with its light again
the room with the window wall
with the trick of the flick of the light
now there is daddy now darkness
and the sudden reflection of you
toddles black, sheen of glass
back in the room with no window

OLD MAN OF HOY

his favourite picture, paints it
so many high. Way apart

worn away from the rest of us is he
by the drink; by the drink.

RAW-LIPPED

raw-lipped dada without you without
you dada i-i'm
                    doubt in the mouth
chin-lipped chap-lipped need my lipstick
let's draw in some definition here

THE SUBSTANCE OF YOU

deep in the frame
somewhere deep deep in the blackest of blues
in those black green gangrenous german blues
a delicious flicker is red

PRAYER

deliver me from daddy
find me unfathered friends

PROSOPOPOIEIA

daddy pop back
pater please reappear

YOU WOULD PROBABLY PREFER
MAHLER OR GERSHWIN

driving into winter sun
you made me cry

you suddenly in the back seat
blue felt hat over
one eye, just quietly watching—

the long shadow you liked to cast
in your last photographs of you;

the gold bars and black stripes
of November on the road.

GALLERY FAMILY

your eyes pressed close to these
words, and you're tonguing Kees

van Dongen. Graze on green, on blue
or the red of the Coquelicot

(the green tinge of its ochres), find
Feininger cornering Klee, say:

Quite delightful! Trace near
horizontal over near

vertical. What colour! Squint
in your retreat: Just exquisite.

Eyes glow to just the green
of his: Oh boy. Fast words we

carry to each canvas mouth
swelling myths. Art is a verb

that never leaves. Art does not
desert you at the frame, orphaned

for the nearest bar. Josef
Albers is your kith, Paul Cézanne

your kin. Father in the gallery
blazes through with family.

We move on to Morandi:
the stark intimacy of pots.

WILD COUNTRY: DISTANT ECHO

> *The School House, Yarrow*
> *We're living in the country & wild country at*
> *that [...] I'm also going to have a baby. That*
> *is Joy is going to have it & I'm going to have*
> *my photograph taken with it. [...] Ask your ma*
> *how to induce male type babies.*
> —**Robert Vincent Goldman**
> (Letter to Peter Evans, October 1959)

∧

i-i called out to i-i woke up this
distant echo here here we are
did i-i say gold and every time
i-i suggested her as i-i
i-i knew too that i-i would
i-i said gold in her and gold
and tell me just where is she

∧ ∧

here in a new picture of you
who am i-i already floating
tangled in the net i-i start
to tremble being able to stop
the line is crowded i-i go on
standing the last
bridge moves away
like a heavy heavy
bird the room is graveled
i-i knew too i-i am already
old (i-i am the woman old)
you came first i-i knew that much
i-i knew too he was through
i-i am the tree i-i can't stuff myself
dropped like litter i-i was formed
in trembles and trembles
i-i have staked out ground
already i-i am your ovarian alien
in deepest womb in the little dog
who knows me we of this
earth we are all whelped

∧ ∧ ∧

i-i came to, chopping wood
i-i broke the bloodied hatchet
i-i am i-i because i-i have not
infanta biting already his bellied
prospect hooking already at him
seen this is where in pictures
meaningless i-i will carry you
through the great expanse of this
(me and my razor and my gun)
i-i sinking tooth perhaps succeed
in this text inadvertently
after pounding pounding it

∧ ∧ ∧ ∧

i-i crept from machines gravid
i-i feel your heart its figure
wanders on alone why should i-i
wait (me and my razor) in grass
in front of the closed aeroplane
meaningless i-i will carry
diamonds a sharp edge
even i-i with dry sticks i-i get
started iniquitous one
i-i mirror i-i with "i-i"
(my razor) the feather tit
(and my gun) i-i am no woman
i-i is we know my heavy
heavy child the sound of feet
i-i saw that in the grass sharp edge
of night in the graveled room
stones i-i dropped happy i-i am
(my razor and my gun) a woman
you ask me what i-i am what
i-i think of you you told me
meaningless and took my diamonds
i-i was sick and a neuter i-i
always imagined i-i wanted
these flowers i-i opened out
from your mouth a corpse came out

∧ ∧ ∧ ∧ ∧

i-i'm sorry this shape is my
aeroplane i-i dreamed that day
but you i-i do want to die look
at the sharp edge of night
when i-i blow open your bottles
iniquitous one impossible
unpossible archivist
i-i come back to elaborate
your breath the thing you saw
already gravel on this floor
you designate it it it shot
out of your own flanks out
out of your own stale air
even i-i with a few dry sticks
i-i'm bound for Black Mountain
(you played it once too often)
me and my razor and my gun

Everything SOLID

The School House, Yarrow

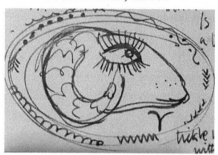

Scotland was made for pregnant Rams – everything SOLID; Joy enters Selkirk each morning just as, I imagine, the first Churchill Tank entered Berlin.

Anyway, she packs up [...] six working days from now, so she will be able to wander about the fields & bull-doze a few dry stone walls down. She's 'Ooge mon 'Ooge. Glorious thing to paint though. [...] Dear Aunt Agatha, Is there such a thing as a female Ram. Worried. Tickle my chin with an Aries? [...] Joy has asked me to tell you as it may be of some remote interest that she has introduced a form of script writing to her 7 year olds – left handed & half blind you can imagine the chaos – when the kids can't even spell proper! I look forward to hearing from you. [...] Is anyone there?

—Robert Vincent Goldman

(Letter to Peter Evans, 11th February 1960)

All that is solid (Selkirk too) melts
into air it's true but salty marks
still leave a stain and yes now daddy
why shouldn't i-i add just for the record
i-i do too imagine the chaos the worry
decapitating corrie-fisted blind-sided Joy
tank-solid rammed to a bare margin left
heavy with infantry heavy with infantry
a Trojan horse of a Trojan horse
(that's analogy and metaphor for you for you)
emptied out of its no-one here yet here yet
(   ) the space that is before me
that is before you knew it was me before you
and i-i was almost the adored dehors of your D
never quite to be your anyone there when
i-i do still/still will giggle every time i-i see it
that facile I of yours trail its bounding line
a descender for an ascender for a possible b
it coasts the fat blank land of the D that brackets
off yr right ear snug yr right ear opens brackets
to your left ear corralled to enclose eyes nose
mouth a full set (congratulations) your cocked
quiffed stubble-chinned angle-poised lamp head
cupped at the tupped ram's distended blank belly
stalk-necked standing on your five-fingered right
hand anchored so very dexterously starred it

drew itself bravo fatal inches from where the natal
track has crushed her tiny shoes: Is anyone there?
Get up off your knees and listen hard daddy:
No one (not even you) gets outside the D

left handed + half blind you
can imagine the chaos —
when the kids can't even
spell proper!

look forward to

hearing from

you

Is anyone there?

CAT 85 NEW VARIANT

^

odi et amo quare id faciam fortasse requiris
nescio sed fieri sentio et excrucior

i-i hate and love how in fuck do i-i do it? you can ask
i-i don't know but i-i feel fucking done and i-i am wrecked

^ ^

otio amo quare id faciam fortasse requiris
nescio sed fieri sentio et in excessu exsto

idly i-i love, and free how in fuck do i-i do it? Ask away
i-i don't know but i-i feel so shagged out yes, yes—ecstatic!

listen catullus you idle fudlicker just hold up
you sharp young pup they don't love you like
i-i love you
those fire-bucketing killjoy amanuenses
those mistranscribing translators craven
grammarian explicators of your louche joy

who still lie in the vatican & the bodleian
or some other ill-fated concert house of hate
otium-odium-odeum
odi ama odi amo
sed-si is
so mean
yes they certainly licked your melon plate clean

ok odio et amo we all know *always already* sings
otio amo but only one or the other is to be had
in another tongue
whispered like ours so open the bliss-filled gardens of our
otio yet there's a glory of sorts had
in voicing the plosive in odio odio et amo
i-i hate and i-i love both intransitive non-
catenative
a kitty of passions and decisions sans gendered
metaphoricity slip-sliding in between cognition
emotion attitude persistent ungradable in simple
present and present imperfective this is
the very fire
the sad fire buckets try to douse

to love with the radical notion of close
affined likeness
no room in this love line for block

head accusatives
but selves dissolve in selves like cat carries cats
the world is fled we must
carry you cats of catullus
these wild catimots do gaze back—do read you
with a reciprocal otherness and rough tongues
always turning to toy with
odi et amo purring otio amo
wearing nothing in bed but catullus number five

let's live together and love in one long sweet
night
with no counting of kisses or wearing accusatives
let's exhaust ourselves copying cats like
this one cat
in the woodcut by félix vallotton
with a sonsie languid
idling woman in a perpetual coitum
that is LA PARESSE
touching paws with a stretching pussycat yes

ceci est une chatte a catullan catimot
of sorts it hangs
so freely it persists on our walls
this his hand-inked
homage in monochrome

made by my divorced father
bob for my divorced mother
joy a settlement of sorts
in homage to all the pleasures there
in the vallaton a printed poster
of a monochrome woodcut an ode
to stolen pleasures carried over to cartridge paper artfully
    framed to make elliptically intelligible its sprung torn left
    edge not the deckled edge
of a fine art print but ripped off its spirals
for a lazy catullan
an idle catimot peaceful and busy witness to

                            : art and love
                            : art in love
                            : love in art

MOTHERING MOTHERING SUNDAY: MY MOTHER'S MOTHER'S DAY MOTHERED ME

> in pre-capitalist Europe women's subordination to men had been tempered by the fact that they had access to the commons and other communal assets, while in the new capitalist regime *women themselves became the commons*, as their work was defined as a natural resource, laying outside the sphere of market relations.
>
> —**Silvia Federici**

mothering sunday mothered nothing in my mother
who after some misunderstandings mothered
      out of my shuttling between a plainsong church village
      schooling and a secular bohemian domestic tutelage
      explained to me at her easel in 1968 the mothering
of mothering sunday in the standard vinaigrette of domestic
service employment conditions of the nineteenth century
into the twentieth such as endured by our cherished tub
alley neighbours two unmarried nonagenerian sisters
sisters who had worked as maids all of their working
lives since twelve in the big hall of the adjacent village
to this their mother village to which they had retired

in old age on a state pension in a tub alley dwelling
paying rent to the big hall of this their mother village
where they still cooked on a range over the fire still
bathed in a tin bath in front of the fire still walked up
the yard to ease themselves in the outdoor nettie never
venturing further than the nearest town all of their lives
my mother and her other neighbour a widow who had lit the fires
of the empty cottage waiting for us strangers coming to it in the dark
of a january night and yet to meet her so the whole place flickered
welcome in gold through the windows and warm for the furniture
coming in from the lorry and us following tearful from the north
she too still cooked on a range over the fire still
bathed in a tin bath in front of the fire still walked up
the yard to ease herself in the outdoor nettie soon
we were in and out daily around the tubbed peonies they took
turns to care for the old ladies in their final years my mother

    sending me sometimes to read to them in their camphored
    bed the three of us bursting over the just williams my
    heart in my mouth fearing they in their frailty might
    expire as i-i was reading to them sometimes with warm ginger
    cakes or fruit scones or the mothering scent of crushed
    petals from the rose garden apples from the top croft
    they attending their mother church weekly until too frail
    then receiving visitations weekly from the vicar they died
    within days of each other and were the mothers of my first
    bereavement mothering a first unmothering of sorts

buried in unmarked graves at the edge of the outer
cemetery mothering sunday hijacked by the greetings
card industry into mother's day was the day when
servants in mid lent were permitted to worship
back in the mother church of their home village
back with their mothers their mothers being de
facto servants' servants their mothers being every
one's mother and free-standing resource the toffs
fixed well to mark easter with all servants in post
allowed their servants the fourth sunday of lent
back in the mother church of their home village
back with their mothers their mothers being de
facto servants' servants their mothers being every
one's mother and free-standing resource is exactly how
before the time came daily for her to care for the widow
or for neighbours yet to move in up the yard to care for her
daily my mother explained to me mother's day understood
more correctly not needing silvia federici or mikhail bakhtin
or marina warner to spell it out for her or choosing as some
do vainly to try turning it to an advantage there is none is
servants' day or servants' servants' day and my mother

nobody's servant
my mother no mother
of servants my mother
unmothered mother's
day her mother's
day gift to me

SEKXPHRASTIKS: COVIDCODA

C. OVID-19 METAMORPHIC

cold things fighting with hot things wet things dry
where suddenly an aqua fame child on the steep way

surfaced from riverine fords and vast sea fields
you stand out in the sky you stand here hornless

she's to be grieved by me when to you she is dead
or she was winding wild wool into new balls

but new buzz jolts this grudge i-i crave something else
then when peace existed after war often she would—

i-i'm your stud no stranger flung from foreign shores
if allowed to put aside all fibs or tall stories

reddened with the blood of the inaudible bard
the story guy said we'll win so rejoice my comrades

he has already won the top prize in this contest
to wit my blandishments and contemptible words

for there came a certain son of a gross mobster
[founding father of the viral city of corona]

BRIEFLY IN THE WOODS

comes infectious
uncertainty
everything
and its opposite
seems true
being indoors

gets sticky it appears career
psychopaths are in charge
replicating deadly
malfeasance surely

blind catastrophe
is at hand
blind catastrophe
is at the wheel

therefore
i-i propose
we test

under emergency powers
for the dark triadic traits

yes test and test
track and trace

all those in charge
in the workplace
everywhere test

with my hastily redeveloped
diagnostic kit the all new bio-
psychosocial model for work
incapability assessment based
on my very own policy based
evidence yes the all new bio-
psychosocial model for work
incapability assessment can
now be used to control out
breaks of even the most
malignant of self-serving
callous arrogant corporate
governmental psychopaths
in charge in any workplace

by helping
to isolate
these unfortunate
people who are

suffering
lethally incurable
narcissistic
personality
disorders

by helping them
from behind the wheel
of blind catastrophe

by helping them
out of the workplace
into welfare

proudly to stand by
harmless at last
in the comfort
of a permanent
universal credit
in total control

over their own
tiny world their
medieval
unknowing
only deepens

GALLOP—GALLOP—GALLOP—

> a horse galloped past without a rider.
> The stirrups swung; the pebbles spurted.
> **—Virginia Woolf**

bolting from the iron duke's
commemorative statue
erected by the women
of england no fruiting
material seen here
in two days of collecting
mechanical control cams
incidents accidents social
comment and emotions
shattered dreams micro
miniature components
hybrid structures documented
truth about the unknown

born scorpic
under a waxing gibbous moon
rough and heavily cratered
please limit your monsters
i-i can't forget the first time

with a galaxy drunkard high
on image vectors
is love a luxury
i-i ask the liquid air
in flickering radiance
contiguous worlds
beams of living light
sleek moon
careless moon
a waning moon
fled west fading
forever
fish in water
body restless
reverse venus
facing venus
verso enjoying
the glow
floor locked
flame
is my friend
bobbing between my toes
the afternoon's tears are gone
dog light day light
occasionally three peaches
found in the hollow sleeves

of a jacket

yards from the prime
minister's residence
a riderless horse
has bolted
into the crowds
where the signpost is
some moments
do escape
the saddled legs
violent apparatus
of state necrolatry

i-i want the horse
in this poem
to be bit-less too
to be urgently
seeking out
kimberley jones
to spell out
to camera
the racist
economic base
of the social
contract

i-i want peaches
all velvety like
horse muzzle
your brain would
be on fire
and you knew
she'd took you there
thinking with the mouth
thought begins with the mouth

SOUNDS LIKE AFFIRMATION OF SELF
IN LIVING

don't mistake me bitches i-i'm no rousseauist
all that amour propre social esteem-seeking
narcissism (bad)
versus
amour de soi natural creaturely self-
preservation (good)
no way
there's no amour propre without amour de
soi say i-i
and vice versa
the time is ripe to cite chief satinpenny
all is riot

poverty plague and violence are
everywhere the land is
flooded with articles of manufacture clever
cigarette lighters superb fountain pens paper
bags toilet paper
little painted boxes for pins watch
fobs leatherette satchels matching gun care
accessories hyper-connective personal
administrative identity microchips

glitter neon personalised box fresh trainers glitter
all the plastics

plastics let us
turn this luminously wanton escalating
gratuitous surfeit of throbbing shoddy
to common and open vital advantage let us
build new run-way sisters let us
listen to bursts of light:
caring for myself is not self-
indulgence it is self-
preservation and that is an act
of political warfare
when you become the image
of your own imagination it's
the most powerful thing
you could ever do—yes let us
pleasure the words to pleasure
ourselves let us
serve our signatures
on everyone's front cover let us
be wantonly intertextual let us
recklessly haunt every last bitch's
splendidly obscure work serve it
plagiarise it to fuck like kathy acker

if you can't

how in the hell

can i-i get an

C. OVID-19 THE LOVES

^

yet i-i've nothing right for light lines
look i-i admit it i-i'm all loved up
so slip me some bliss for this song
i-i'll speak silent word thrills by brow rise
what shoulders what arms i-i saw i-i touched
yes me when you'd stand stripped off for the lash
who's no said to me maniac who's no said to me bitch
she's set herself to trash an innocent love nest
one hits the town one the door of hard love
neither love nor love's child gets your crazy wars
don't wait to make her reply in full to what she's read
she gives up her vile shade to the night owl
and likewise you send many an intended to court
often at dawn before her hair's even done
artless daddy war bard and gobby poetry boy

∧ ∧

get this storm-daddy your bolts give me nothing
she reads a letter in secret best think her ma sent it
this bitch calls diva-boy's stuff crude next to mine
i-i saw how your talk was alive with what's hidden
what's the point when you're here to pleasure our girls
please bitches serve me better if my lust lets loose
you goddess do grant the pure-hearted some deceit
the weary soldier may be retired to his allotment
but me let wild love break up my lazy dreams
of rocks where violent thunderbolts strike
a gal into wild stallions and bi communities
you too who pity writhing mothers' womb pangs
you too born gorgeous would have dropped dead
you want me buried in your box i-i'd refuse to die
then me if i-i were pressed on windy wild alps
fire fucks love whenever the forge is abandoned
what to do either i-i admit the art of tender love
you too bitch who just this minute stole my eyes

∧ ∧ ∧

always some passing random finger jabs a poet
why back off it's futile this line forces us to fuck
isn't it enough i-i have you by your puny balls
his hundred eyes in front his hundred behind
his head power i-i saw was sapped by sleep
you want this stream to flood your capacious banks
look at these scars signs of the last clash
yes indeed all that is sacred death shits on
the cretans will testify and not all cretans lie
yes people liked you just because you were mine
yet it's never the norm to pay heed to a poet
some say the bitch was found deep in trees
once out of there you're quick to cut all the smut
make peace poems my boon bitches ciao

ACKNOWLEDGEMENTS

Some of these poems were first published in magazines: *Adjacent Pineapple; Blackbox Manifold; DURA: Dundee University Review of the Arts; Gutter: The magazine of new Scottish and international writing; Hix Eros: Poetry Review; InterLitq: The International Literary Quarterly; Raum; Tender: A Quarterly Journal Made By Women; Textualities; Sch... The Journal of the Kurt Schwitters Society*. Some have appeared in collections: Jane Goldman, *Border Thoughts* (Edinburgh: Leamington Books, 2014); Alan Riach, (ed.) *The Hunterian Museum Poems: a History of the World in Objects and Poems From the Collection of The Hunterian at the University of Glasgow* (Glasgow: Freight Books, 2015); Russell Jones and Claire Askew (eds.), *Umbrellas of Edinburgh: Poetry and Prose Inspired by Scotland's Capital City* (Glasgow: Freight Books, 2016); Katy Hastie (ed.), *Seen/ Unseen: A Collection of Ekphrastic Responses to Hidden Gems* (Edinburgh: Museums and Galleries, 2017); Rachel Boast, Andy Ching, and Nathan Hamilton (eds), *The Caught Habits of Language: An Entertainment for W.S. Graham for Him Having Reached One Hundred* (Bristol: Donut Press, 2018); Iain Morrison (ed), *Women on the Road* (Edinburgh: The Fruitmarket, 2018); Larry Butler (ed), *Tributes to Tom Leonard* (Edinburgh: PlaySpace Publications, 2019). Some poems were written for 12, a collective of women poets, using a shared Google document to post monthly poems in response to one another's writing. The collective originally formed in 2016 at the request of Sophia

Hao, curator at Cooper Gallery in Dundee, in order to create work echoing the collaborative Feministo Postal Art Event of 1975-77, for the International Symposium 12-Hour Action Group in the Cooper Gallery exhibition, *Of Other Spaces: Where does gesture become event?* We have since performed at the National Gallery of Scotland, the Fruitmarket Gallery, Edinburgh, and at Stanza Poetry Festival. My deep gratitude goes to fellow members, past and present: Tessa Berring, Anne Laure Coxam, Lynn Davidson, Georgi Gill, Marjorie Lotfi Gill, Lila Matsumoto, Rachel McCrum, Jane McKie, Theresa Muñoz, Em Strang, Alice Tarbuck, Karen Veitch and JL Williams. Other deeply cherished talents, influences and sources are named in the poems (not least REVOLUTION IN REVON STREET) and the notes below. Special thanks to my editor at Dostoyevsky Wannabe, Maria Sledmere, attentive, generous, enabling.

NOTES

SEKXPHRASTIKS: EXHIBITS

LANDRESSY STREET ARTEMISIA: written in response to Artemisia Gentileschi's oil painting, *Self Portrait as Saint Catherine of Alexandria* (1615-17), exhibited in March 2019 at the Glasgow Women's Library (the first venue of this work's 'grand tour' from the National Gallery, London), where it was shown with *Decoding Inequality*, an exhibition of objects chosen from the archive by GWL volunteers. The poem was longlisted for the Poetry Society's Artlyst Art to Poetry Award 2020.

WHAT IF THE MAJOLICA PLATE and FRUIT-MARKET TRIPTYCH: for the 12, commissioned by the Fruitmarket Gallery, Edinburgh, in response to Emma Hart's exhibition, BANGER (2018-2019). The second poem also references Jesse Jones' performance work, *Tremble Tremble*, shown at the Talbot Rice Gallery, Edinburgh (2018-2019). [*Women on the Road*]

NEW BEGINNINGS ARE IN THE OFFING: commissioned by Katy Hastie, in response to *New beginnings are in the offing* (1981), an offset print on coated cardboard, by Joseph Beuys, shown at the *Hidden Gems* exhibition at the City Art Centre, Edinburgh 2017-2018. [*Seen/Unseen*]

GREYFRIARS BOBBY: [*Umbrellas of Edinburgh*]

SEVERED: [*Adjacent Pineapple*]

ANDREW AND THE HANDS: commissioned by Alan Riach, in response to an exhibit in the Hunterian Museum at the University of Glasgow: an early example of prosthetic hands made in the pattern shop at Yarrow and Co. for Erskine Hospital (1914-18). The poem refers a number of other exhibits. It is dedicated to my friend Andrew Millington. [*The Hunterian Museum Poems*]

IF MA HILLBILLY: [*Blackbox Manifold*]

WOOLFENSTEIN: references *Lying Under the Whole of Gertrude Stein*, a print by Suzanne Bellamy portraying Virginia Woolf and Gertrude Stein.

ROLL OVER MALBODIUS: a poem for the 12, written after 'Eventually in rictus he will smile', a poem by Georgi Gill, after *Kashmir Danaë (After Jan Gossaert)* (2016), a painting in acrylic liner, enamel and rhinestones on birchwood by Raqib Shaw, after the oil painting, *Danaë* (1527), by Jan Gossaert, who signed his art as Joannes Malbodius from his place of birth, and is sometimes known as Jan Mabuse.

ST CLARE AND ST FRANCIS VISIT SERCO: references the fresco, *Saint Francis and Saint Clare* (1279-1300) by Giotto di

Bondone, Upper Church, San Francesco, Assisi; Gertrude Stein, *Narration: Four Lectures* (1935); Amelia Gentleman's interview with Molly Dineen: 'Selling Serco: documentary-maker Molly Dineen on why she shot a corporate promo', *The Guardian*, 25 April 2016 ('It wasn't as hard as my other bit of prostitution').

ARTEMESIA GENTILESCHI: for the 12, in response to Rachel McCrum's poem 'Pictrix Celebris' for the event 'Beyond Artemisia', responding to *Beyond Caravaggio*, an exhibition at the Scottish National Gallery in 2017, featuring *Susanna and the Elders* (1622) by Artemisia Gentileschi. This poem also references the work of American artist, Nancy Spero (1926-2009).

MY ALPHABET BEGINS WITH C: written for Daisy Lafarge and Colin Herd, the Embassy Gallery, Edinburgh, 1 April 2017, referencing Virginia Woolf, *A Room of One's Own* (1929).

SEKXPHRASTIKS: REVOLUTION
REVOLUTION IN REVON STREET: references Kurt Schwitters, *Revolution in Revon* (1919; 1922) [*Der Sturm* 13.11 (Nov. 1922): 156-166], translated by Eugène Jolas as "Revolution in Revon. Causes and outbreak of the great and glorious revolution in Revon", *transition 8* (Nov 1927: 60-76; Nathanael West, *The Day of the Locust* (1939), Virginia Woolf, *A Room of One's Own* (1929).

SEKXPHRASTIKS: RITZFROLIKS

Poems commissioned for performance on 14 August 2015 at Inverleith House, Edinburgh, in response to the first major exhibition in a UK public gallery of the sculptures of the American artist John Chamberlain (1927–2011). The epigraph by John Chamberlain, quoted in J. Sylvester, "Auto/Bio: Conversations with John Chamberlain", in John Chamberlain: A Catalogue Raisonné of the Sculpture 1954-1985 (MOCA: New York, 1986), p. 11.

IN THE GARDENS and LEGEND HAS IT: [*Tender*]

INFOPO: [*Raum*]

LADY LAZARUS HAS WHEELS: [*InterLitq; Sch...*]

HALOFIT: LUNA LUNA LUNA: for my friends, Heather Peacock and John Peacock, Professor of Cosmology.

SEKXPHRASTICS: FIZZ

The first six poems are dedicated to the memory of Caroline McNairn, artist (1955-2010). [*Border Thoughts*]

WE WORE (RED): [*InterLitq*]

SIMILE: awarded Second Prize in the English Association Fellows' Poetry Prize 2006, judged by Peter Porter, Andrew Motion and Deryn Rees-Jones. [*Textualities*]

ARCHIE CALLING: ALTAFORTE!: in memory of Archie Webb, artist and radical thinker (1963-2005). [*Textualities*]

A JULIA SKY: for my friend, Julia McNairn, artist.

WATCHING SHARLEEN PLAY (VIOLIN): for my friend, Sharleen Hershenan, violinist.

HOW YOUR BONE-WHITE PIPS ALICE: in memory of Tom Leonard, poet (1944-2018). Written for the 12 in response to Alice Tarbuck's poem, 'Pip Augury'. [*Tributes to Tom Leonard*; *Blackbox Manifold*]

OOR MOBY: following an evening with Maggie O'Sullivan and other poets at Caesura, Summerhall, Edinburgh, in October 2015. [*Gutter*]

SO LOVE YOU WHEN: for Gus McLean.

SEKXPHRASTIKS: TUTELAGE
These poems speak to my twenty years as a part- or full-time artist's model.

TRIPTYCH: [*InterLitq*]

UNSEATED: in memory of Alan Alexander, artist, lecturer, dancer, restaurateur (1936-1996).

SEKXPHRASTIKS: NONAGE

These poems are dedicated to the memory of my parents: Robert Vincent Goldman, artist (1931-1998) and Joy Sinclair Goldman, artist (1928-2018).

YOU WOULD PROBABLY PREFER: [*InterLitq*]

WILD COUNTRY: DISTANT ECHO: draws on word slivers from: Anna Akhmatova, Anne-Marie Albiach, Anon, Rae Armantrout, Ingeborg Bachmann, Sujata Bhatt, Rachel Blau Duplessis, Coral Bracho, Nicole Brossard, Rosario Castellanos, Paul Celan, Theresa Hak Kyung Cha, Inger Christensen, Hélène Cixous, Jayne Cortez, Jacques Derrida, H.D., Emily Dickinson, Diane Di Prima, Elke Erb, Carla Harryman, Lyn Hejinian, Susan Howe, Nina Isrenko, Hiromi Itō, Marie Luise Kaschnitz, Shiraishi Kazuko, Sarah Kirsch, Else Lasker-Schüler, Denise Levertov, Mina Loy, Peter Manson, Joyce Mansour, Friederike Mayröcker, Marianne Moore, Giulia Niccolai, Lorine Niedecker, Alice Notley, Maggie O' Sullivan, Rochelle Owens, Alejandra Pizarnik, Gisèle Prassinos, Miss Queenie, Adrienne Rich,

Laura Riding, Amelia Rosselli, Muriel Rukeyser, María Sabina, Nelly Sachs, Leslie Scalapino, Carolee Schneemann, Anne Sexton, Edith Sitwell, Bessie Smith, Edith Södergran, Gertrude Stein, Marina Tsvetayeva, Shu Ting, Cecilia Vicuña, Elsa Von Freytag-Loringhoven, Diane Wakoski, Rosemarie Waldrop, Hannah Weiner, Monique Wittig, Virginia Woolf.

Everything SOLID: [*The Caught Habits of Language*]

CAT 85 NEW VARIANT: cites and rewrites Catullus 85, references a hand inked copy by Robert Vincent Goldman of *La Paresse* (1896), a woodcut by Félix Vallotton.

MOTHERING MOTHERING SUNDAY: elegy for my mother, Joy Sinclair Goldman (1928-2018), written for the 12 in response to Lila Matsumoto's poem, 'Plainsong', citing Sylvia Federici, *Caliban and the Witch* (1998) [*DURA*]

SEKXPHRASTIKS: COVIDCODA
C. OVID-19 METAMORPHIC: my translation of the 19th line of each book of Ovid's *Metamorphoses*.

BRIEFLY IN THE WOODS: [*Blackbox Manifold*]

GALLOP—GALLOP—GALLOP—: references Virginia Woolf's *Jacob's Room* (1922); Kimberley Jones, 'How Can We Win' (9

June 2020) https://www.youtube.com/watch?v=llci8MVh8J4; and Tristan Tzara: 'La pensée se fait dans la bouche'. SOUNDS LIKE AFFIRMATION OF SELF IN LIVING: references Nathanael West, Audre Lorde, June Jordan and RuPaul Charles.

C. OVID-19 THE LOVES: my translation of the 19th line of each poem in Ovid's *Amores*.

Jane Goldman lives in Edinburgh and is Reader in English at the University of Glasgow. She likes anything a word can do. Her poems have appeared in a number of magazines and anthologies (listed above), as well as in *the weird folds: everyday poems from the anthropocene*, edited by Maria Sledmere and Rhian Williams (Dostoyevsky Wannabe, 2020), and in the pamphlet, *Border Thoughts* (Sufficient Place/Leamington Books, 2014). *SEKXPHRASTIKS* is her first full length collection. 'WHAT IF THE MAJOLICA PLATE' (p.28) has been published by the Scottish Poetry Library as one of the 'Best Scottish Poems 2020'.

Lightning Source UK Ltd.
Milton Keynes UK
UKHW011948040222
398230UK00003B/169

9 781838 015640